Issues of the Heart

Devotional

LISA SINGH

Issues of the Heart

Copyright © 2017 Inspirations by Lisa

DEDICATION

This book is dedicated firstly to my Lord and Savior Jesus Christ who has given me a second chance in life. I would also like to dedicate this book to my team that worked tirelessly to make this book a reality and finally to you the reader. May Grace and Peace be multiplied to you through Jesus Christ our Lord!

TABLE OF CONTENTS

INTRODUCTION

It has always been my desire as far as I could remember to put together a devotional that would help people grow in their spiritual walk with God. I have also started many devotional projects that just never seemed to capture the heart of my desire until now. This devotional is not only a one a day read, but it takes time to focus on *issues of the heart* ranging from four to seven days per topic. I love to teach God's word because teaching is a gift God has given to leaders with a strong desire to see their people grow healthy. Teaching requires a commitment of heart to God's people even when we can't see the fruit forthcoming.

Over the past seven years, I have learned the responsibility of teaching God's word whether I had seven or fifty people in my congregation because I know every time I teach God's word I am seeding the heart of God's people. Because of my commitment to teaching, I have organized short devotionals in one book; they are compilations of the sermons I have taught my local congregation over the past several years.

Issues of the heart is a precious piece of work to my heart because every devotion you will read was birthed out of a place of learning on my journey with God. Every topic and every day you read this devotional I want you to remember I wrote from the place where I was in life. God is so concerned about our heart condition. I spent a lot of years pretending and beautifying my external image, but inside I was decaying. God said, "I will give you a new heart and put a new spirit in you; I will remove from you your heart of stone and give you a heart of flesh." (Ezekiel 36:26 NIV). And King Solomon told us, "Above all else, guard your heart, for everything you do flows from it." (Proverbs 4:23 NIV). The heart is so important in the natural because once our hearts stop beating, we shut down; just as the heart is so essential to natural life, the new heart that God has given us at salvation is just as important to our spiritual life. Everything we do flows from the inner man, and God looks at the inner man to see the intentions and desires buried within.

We live in a world that teaches us to express our true selves yet the culture of the day seems to dictate who we should be, and because of trying to fit in and keep up, we live from a place of superficiality. We use fashion, the cars we drive, the places and the people we hang out with as a gauge for true happiness and identity; yet when we are alone, our heart aches and longs to be free from the bondages that consume our inner core. God said to Isaiah, "These people come near to me with their mouth and honor me with their lips, but their hearts are far from me. Their worship of me is based on merely human rules they have been taught." Isaiah 29:13 (NIV)

God cuts through all the layers of our lives, and he gets to the heart and every day though we know the Lord loves us, we know his word. We go to church every time the doors are opened, we watch Christian television, and we listen to worship music, but somehow we still find our hearts troubled. We struggle daily with Issues of the heart, we can't let go of the past, we allow the hurts, pain, and disappointments in life to stunt our growth and kill our dreams, our lives seem to be a constant storm, and we just live defeated. I want to encourage you to take your time and go through this devotional because I know God will speak to your heart every day and healing will begin. At the end of every plan, I have provided a place for reflections so you can express the issues of your heart. God has heard your cry, and he wants you to live from a place of victory, so open up your heart to him and let him bring you to a place of authenticity; let him deal with the "*Issues of your heart!*"

Plan 1

CREATED ON PURPOSE FOR PURPOSE

==

You were created for Purpose; God's Purpose! Uniquely gifted and designed to fulfill his purposes in your life. Everyone has a sense that they were born for a purpose, but there is something more than just a purpose. The God purpose was specifically designed for you. And it is your responsibility to live out God's plan for you, becoming his masterpiece.

DAY 1

God Does Not Create Anything Insignificant, Inferior, Or Without A Purpose

In the Christian circle, purpose is a word that is frequently used, yet to me, it was just a word. However, if we are to get where we are going in this life, purpose is the defining factor in the end result. On my new venture with my heavenly father, I began to get the clarity necessary for a successful journey and slowly realized the whole point of getting saved was not just to secure a spot in heaven when the Lord returns, but more so that I would be a living testimony for Jesus Christ.

Life is more than just passing through to get to a better place; even though that will be the end result, we have to believe that life is much more and that the reason we were put on the earth is not to do time or to buy time but accomplish something with the time we have been given. We have to arrive at a place in our lives where we are convinced beyond the shadow of a doubt that we have been created on purpose for purpose!

"On purpose" means intentional or deliberate. God's plan for creating us was intentional and deliberate, and there had to be a process of planning which would have crystallized the details for the finished product. My friends, I want to make this statement a personal one as you say it out loud so you can hear yourself, "I am created on purpose for purpose!"

Power Thought: *I don't just have a purpose, but I have a God-purpose.*

DAILY SCRIPTURES FOR MEDITATION

God said, Let Us [Father, Son, and Holy Spirit] make mankind in Our image, after Our likeness, and let them have complete authority over the fish of the sea, the birds of the air, the [tame] beasts, and over all of the earth, and over everything that creeps upon the earth. So God created man in His own image, the image and likeness of God He created him; male and female He created them. And God blessed them and said to them, Be fruitful, multiply, and fill the earth, and subdue it [using all its vast resources in the service of God and man]; and have dominion over the fish of the sea, the birds of the air, and over every living creature that moves upon the earth. - Genesis 1:26-28 (AMP)

DAY 2

What Is Our God Purpose?

We have all been equipped with certain gifts and talents by God to accomplish our purpose, and it all leads to one specific end, and that is to be a witness for him. Every one of us was created to be a witness for Jesus.

It does not mean that once we become a Christian that we have to leave our jobs and families and go off on some mission to a country to help the poor. While helping poor people should be our concern and considering the experience of a mission trip in the future could prove beneficial to our worldview of poverty. God does not expect us to leave life as we know it unless there is a specific call on our lives for missions. But his purpose is for us to use the platform we have been given through our talents and gifting to be a witness right where we are. So it doesn't matter what field we may be in, the fact is, this specific field now transforms into a witnessing field.

The idea is that while we are operating in our purpose in life, we are fulfilling the God purpose by using our natural talents, such as leadership skills, artistic skills, compassion, kindness, and even encouragement to glorify God and lead others to him.

As believers, we need to have a revelation that this time on earth is only as it suggests- for a time, and then there is life after, but while here, God wants us to be good stewards of time!

Power Thought: *My ultimate God-purpose is to be a witness for God.*

DAILY SCRIPTURES FOR MEDITATION

"But you shall receive power (ability, efficiency, and might) when the Holy Spirit has come upon you, and you shall be My witnesses in Jerusalem and all Judea and Samaria and to the ends (the very bounds) of the earth." - Acts 1:8 (AMPC)

DAY 3

Reconstruction Is A Very Necessary Part Of Fulfilling The God Purpose In Our Lives.

At the point of getting saved or being born again, Jesus comes into our lives and takes up residence with our spirit man. The old order and way of thinking must change. When we think about reconstructing something, we get the picture of an already present structure- let's take for example a house that has been abandoned. It may look like a house, but because of neglect or lack of permanent occupants, there may be cracks and holes that developed, there may be rodents and water leaks that leave stains on the floor and walls. The good news is that someone came along, saw the house, thought to themselves that there is potential for this house and it can become livable again. That person did not see the present state but chose to look at what could be.

My friends our bodies are the house; our soul is the inside of the house, and our spirit is where the Holy Spirit takes up residence. Jesus came along and saw what we could be like if he were to move into our lives. He saw the potential of us becoming clean and healthy once he moved into our spirits and he also brought with him every single tool and resource necessary for us to clean up the rest of our house (soul).

In reality, the true source of many of our problems as believers is the fact that we are putting on pretty coats of paint on the outside trying to convince everyone else that we have it all together. Our thought life is so powerful that it could decide our present disposition in life and also determine the direction of our future. Pondering the power of our thought life should cause us to want to reconstruct our souls. We all have a soul, but it is not enough to have a soul; as believers, we should desire a prosperous soul after all the Bible tells us that we are what we think upon, " For as he thinks in his heart, so is he." (Proverbs 23:7 NKJV) and There is only one thing that can truly reconstruct the thought life, and that is the word of God!

Power Thought: *I am made in the image of God, and I consist of spirit, soul, and body.*

DAILY SCRIPTURES FOR MEDITATION

"Beloved I pray that you may prosper in all things and be in health, just as your soul prospers." - 3 John1:2 (NIV)

But God's free gift is not at all to be compared to the trespass [His grace is out of all proportion to the fall of man]. For if many died through one man's falling away (his lapse, his offense), much more profusely did God's grace and the free gift [that comes] through the undeserved favor of the one Man Jesus Christ abound and overflow to and for [the benefit of] many. - Romans 5:15 (AMPC)

DAY 4

How Do We Change Our Thought Patterns?

When we speak about changing our minds, it carries with it the connotation of something existing permanently, but the content changes. For example, your skull contains your brain, and your brain contains your thoughts. You cannot go to the store and buy a new skull with a new brain; you take the permanent skull and brain, and you change the thought patterns that are there. This term is also called repentance.

Repent means to perceive afterward; hence, it signifies to change one's mind or purpose, and it always involves a change for the better. From the definition of repentance, we can now fully understand Rom 12:2 – renewing the mind for the better life God originally had for us.

Many times believers walk away disappointed and frustrated because they want things done instantly. It is almost as if we live in the microwave age, and everything must happen quickly and instantly, or else it is not God. On the contrary, God is here to stay in our lives, and renewing our minds involves building, setting foundation, and then building layer upon layer that causes what we build to remain.

Key: You will have to disconnect from doing things the old way – according to the world system

If we are going to have a prosperous mind, we have to change our habits. Making a few adjustments would only benefit us in the long run. It is the bigger picture that enables us to embrace the changes that need to be implemented because we are now working toward fulfilling the God-purpose for our lives. It is the bigger picture that enables us to embrace the changes that need to be implemented because we are now working toward fulfilling the God-purpose for our lives

Power Thought: *Today I will repent – I will change my mind for the better.*

DAILY SCRIPTURES FOR MEDITATION

Do not be conformed to this world (this age), [fashioned after and adapted to its external, superficial customs], but be transformed (changed) by the [entire] renewal of your mind [by its new ideals and its new attitude], so that you may prove [for yourselves] what is the good and acceptable and perfect will of God, even the thing which is good and acceptable and perfect [in His sight for you]. - Romans 12:2 (AMPC)

DAY 5

Establishing A Sound Mind

Meditation on God's Word is the foundation to a successful life. Our main focus and pursuit must be the Word of God. The main reason our lives should revolve around the Word of God is that the Word is actually our life source that feeds us, nourishes us, and causes us to be healthy in our soul.

There should be no doubts in our minds that the Word of God is Jesus Christ, and that is why our focus is on the Word. When we read the Word of God, we see Jesus in it, and when we see him we are able to see the pattern for our lives. In order for our God-purpose to come to fruition, we must be able to maintain the mind of Christ, and as his mind is formed in us we would then be fully able to manifest his presence to the world.

A constant input of the Word himself – a constant looking to Jesus and his kindness, goodness, love, and mercy toward us – will keep us in a balanced and humble place, and this place is actually where we will be able to release the life-giving Word to others that will affect change.

My friends, there is no other way to be reconstructed, renewed, or transformed but by and through the Word of God.

The Word of God gives life. According to John 10:10 (NIV); Our Savior is life-giving, and once we are connected to him, that very same life should be flowing to us and through us to others.

I love the fact that Jesus did not come just to give life for existence sake, but he describes it as abundant life, an overflowing life, a more than enough life, and this kind of life shows and speaks volumes to the world that he is alive and well.

Power Thought: *Jesus is the Word of God, and I look to him to be transformed.*

DAILY SCRIPTURES FOR MEDITATION

In the beginning [before all time] was the Word (Christ), and the Word was with God, and the Word was God [b]Himself. - John 1:1 (AMPC)

The thief comes only in order to steal and kill and destroy. I came that they may have and enjoy life, and have it in abundance (to the full, till it overflows). - John 10:10 (AMPC)

Reflections

Plan 2

DARE TO DREAM AGAIN

==

"Dream"- what a simple, yet powerful word. As we mature in life, our dreams take the back seat of our lives due to many circumstances that life throws our way. Dreams are given by God, and as a believer, a specific God dream was deposited into each of us to fulfill on the earth. After completing this plan, I pray that your imagination would run wild with the dream God has for you.

Day 1

Dreamers Own The Future

"The future belongs to those who believe in the beauty of their dreams." Eleanor Roosevelt

It is one thing to dream, but it is an entirely different thing to see your dream become a reality. Children have a way of dreaming big, and even in their daydreaming, they can create a world where they can be anyone they want to be. I remember as a child I had the wildest imaginations; I think it was because I did not have the best childhood so these imaginations would take me into a world where I was in control, in charge and safe. I dreamt of being a beauty queen, and in my dreams, I would always win, but as I grew up the realities of life stifled the chance of winning at anything. I know many of you can relate to my story because God created us with an imagination so he can give us the blueprint of our lives. The enemy of our soul knows that God will write his plans in our imagination, so he works tirelessly to ensure that we stop dreaming and believing God for a good future. He brings pressures, disappointments and even potential failures to deter us from the beautiful future God has planned for us.

The Apostle Paul knew of the lies the enemy would use to infiltrate into our minds so he specifically prayed for the church in Ephesus that the eyes of their heart (imagination) would be enlightened and they might know what beautiful things God has in store for them. Note he prays for the eyes of the imagination to be enlightened because that is where God writes his plans for us. Part of the New Covenant involves dreams and visions because God wants his children dreaming again and believing him for the impossible.

The world will risk it all to go after their dreams while the children of God pine away letting fear of failure, disappointments, and obstacles kill their dreams. God wants to write on your hearts the plans he has for you; why not become like a child again, dream again, and believe again, it is never too late. Dale Turner said, *"Dreams are renewable. No matter what our age or condition, there are still untapped possibilities within us and new beauty waiting to be born."* Only you can resurrect those God-given dreams helped by the Holy Spirit and make your future beautiful.

Prayer: *Lord, help me today to dream again. Holy Spirit, please remind me of the plans Abba has for my future. Amen*

DAILY SCRIPTURES FOR MEDITATION

The Day of the Lord
"And afterward, I will pour out my Spirit on all people. Your sons and daughters will prophesy, your old men will dream dreams, your young men will see visions." Even on my servants, both men, and women, I will pour out my Spirit in those days. - Joel 2:28-29 (NIV)

This is the covenant I will establish with the people of Israel after that time declares the Lord. I will put my laws in their minds and write them on their hearts. I will be their God, and they will be my people. - Hebrews 8:10 (NIV)

I pray that the eyes of your heart may be enlightened so you may know the hope to which He has called you, the riches of his glorious inheritance in his holy people. - Ephesians 1:18 (NIV)

Day 2

Dream Killers

*"Never give up on what you really want to do. The person
with big dreams is more powerful than one with all the facts."*
Albert Einstein

In the Bible, we read about a young man named Joseph, and I am
sure many of you are very familiar with him. He was one of Jacob's
sons, and God had a special call on his life. His father loved him and
favored him by giving him a coat of many colors. This made his
brothers very jealous and angry that they hated him. God spoke to
Joseph in a dream showing him the plans for the future; I guess Joseph
was naive in thinking his brothers loved him and he shared his dream
with them which only angered them more.

Today we still have circumstances of jealousy and anger among
family members, friends, peers, and co-workers. The enemy thrives
on bringing distractions like jealousy and hatred for the believer to
abort their God-dream. We should be mindful of who we are sharing
our dreams with because not everyone will celebrate with us.

God had a great plan for Joseph's life, and God reiterated his plan
by giving Joseph this reoccurring dream that one day his family would
bow down to him. Let me just say that if you keep having a dream or
vision that seems similar every time, it may be a sign that God is
showing you the plans for the future. Joseph again shared his dream
with his brothers and father which further incited them to anger.
Little did Joseph know the fate that would befall him due to the
jealousy of the "dream killers"!

Remember that God gives us dreams so we may see hope for our
future but dreams also become fuel to keep going forward even when
we see nothing happening or even when things seem to work against
that dream. God showed Joseph the final outcome of his life in his
dream, but God didn't tell Joseph much detail about his journey to the
final result. The enemy will plant dream killers along the path who
will encourage you to give up but don't blame them sometimes they
do not understand they're being used to keep you back. Say a prayer
for them and leave it in the hands of God, stay focused on what God

has shown you because your dream will take you through many difficult times.

Prayer: *Lord, help me to not focus on the dream killers but to stay focus on the dream you have given me. Amen*

DAILY SCRIPTURES FOR MEDITATION

Now Israel loved Joseph more than any of his other sons, because he had been born to him in his old age; and he made an ornate robe for him.
When his brothers saw that their father loved him more than any of them, they hated him and could not speak a kind word to him. - Genesis 37:3-4 (NIV)

Joseph had a dream, and when he told it to his brothers, they hated him all the more.
He said to them, "Listen to this dream I had:
We were binding sheaves of grain out in the field when suddenly my sheaf rose and stood upright, while your sheaves gathered around mine and bowed down to it."
His brothers said to him, "Do you intend to reign over us? Will you actually rule us?" And they hated him all the more because of his dream and what he had said. - Genesis 37:5 - 8 (NIV)

Then he had another dream, and he told it to his brothers. "Listen," he said, "I had another dream, and this time the sun and moon and eleven stars were bowing down to me."
When he told his father and his brothers, his father rebuked him and said, "What is this dream you had? Will your mother and I and your brothers actually come and bow down to the ground before you?"
His brothers were jealous of him, but his father kept the matter in mind. - Genesis 37:9 -11 (NIV)

Day 3

Dreamers Overcome Hopelessness

"A great leader's courage to fulfill his vision comes from passion, not position." John Maxwell

Thinking about Joseph being their leader, his brothers plotted and planned to ensure it would never become a reality. The Bible tells us they intended to kill him, but one of his brothers named Reuben reasoned with them not to kill him but throw him in a pit with hope to rescue him after and they agreed. Jesus is always praying for us against the dream killers. When we get hold of a God-dream, we literally become a moving target for the enemy because the God-dream prospers not only us but makes way for even generations and nations to be blessed. There is no way the enemy wants the God-dreamer to make it to the end, and so to abort our dreams, he will set up obstacles and hindrances to keep us from seeing it become a reality.

Joseph had the end-result from God-he would be a great leader, and his family would one day bow down to him. As the journey to fulfilling his dream begins it is not without major obstacles:

1. He was stripped of his coat of many colors; his identity was challenged because his coat showed him favored by his father.

2. He was thrown into a pit; left in a place of loneliness, seclusion and given the opportunity to introspect. The enemy majors in getting us alone so he can further drive us to despair so we can abandon our dreams.

3. He was sold as a slave; his dream was challenged when he became the one to serve rather than being served as he had seen in his dream.

I am sure Joseph did not see these obstacles in his journey to leadership, yet it was the reality, and the dream kept him going in the challenging times. His God-dream became the fuel in his hopelessness. His passion for life drove him to never give up on what God had shown him for his future. I am not sure what obstacles may be standing in your way today but like Joseph may you find the passion, to keep on pressing through until your dreams become a reality.

Prayer: *Lord, help me today to find the courage like Joseph did when he faced obstacles to press through to my God-dream. Amen*

DAILY SCRIPTURES FOR MEDITATION

"Here comes that dreamer!" they said to each other. "Come now, let's kill him and throw him into one of these cisterns and say that a ferocious animal devoured him. Then we'll see what comes of his dreams."
When Reuben heard this, he tried to rescue him from their hands. "Let's not take his life," he said. "Don't shed any blood. Throw him into this cistern here in the wilderness, but don't lay a hand on him." Reuben said this to rescue him from them and take him back to his father. - Genesis 37:19 - 21 (NIV)

So when Joseph came to his brothers, they stripped him of his robe— the ornate robe he was wearing— and they took him and threw him into the cistern. The cistern was empty; there was no water in it.
As they sat down to eat their meal, they looked up and saw a caravan of Ishmaelites coming from Gilead. Their camels were loaded with spices, balm, and myrrh, and they were on their way to take them down to Egypt. - Genesis 37:23 - 25 (NIV)

Judah said to his brothers, "What will we gain if we kill our brother and cover up his blood? Come, let's sell him to the Ishmaelites and not lay our hands on him; after all, he is our brother, our own flesh, and blood." His brothers agreed.
So when the Midianite merchants came by, his brothers pulled Joseph up out of the cistern and sold him for twenty shekels of silver to the Ishmaelites, who took him to Egypt. -Genesis 37:26 - 28 (NIV)

Day 4

Dreamers Are Rich

"A poor man is not the one without a cent. A poor man is the one without a dream." Henry Ford

After reading about the challenges Joseph faced I think I might have given up right in the pit, but here we see the power of a God-dream that has taken hold of a life that believes in the one who gave him the dream.

Often we don't recognize that God is all the while stirring our hearts with his desires. The Apostle Paul tells us in the book of Philippians that when our dream comes from God, he will empower us to see it through.

Joseph's life continued to take many twists and turns as he lived in Egypt and the only thing he had in his possession was the God-dream. Joseph goes from the pit to the palace; he landed a job at the home of one of the high ranking officials to Pharaoh. It finally seemed like this dream was about to come to pass but the saga continued in Joseph's life. Potiphar's wife had her eye on Joseph, and she wanted him as her prize, you see, when you are focused on accomplishing the will of God there will always be temptations presented to you to take you off track. Even Jesus faced temptations while fulfilling His God-dream in the wilderness but his resolve to do the will of the father was more important than gaining the world.

A believer with a God-dream can always say, "NO" to the world system. Joseph probably could have gotten to a higher position faster had he taken the opportunity to sleep with his master's wife. But, his knowledge, fear, and love for the God who gave him the dream were greater than the opportunity to satisfy his flesh and so his decision to say no lands him in prison. Joseph is now faced with the reality again that the dream God gave him may never come through yet the story tells us that even in prison he found favor with the prison warden. Joseph's passion for life and his dream practically made his environment come alive, and he seemed to be the wealthiest individual in the world even without money.

Even in prison, God orchestrated a way for Joseph to see his dream become a reality. I believe because Joseph never let his circumstances, obstacles and disappointments kill his confidence in God; he would soon stand before the most powerful man of his time (Pharaoh) and be able to shine.

Prayer: *Lord, help me today to believe the dream you have given me even though I have experienced setbacks and obstacles. Amen*

DAILY SCRIPTURES FOR MEDITATION

So Potiphar left everything he had in Joseph's care; with Joseph in charge, he did not concern himself with anything except the food he ate.
Now Joseph was well-built and handsome, and after a while, his master's wife took notice of Joseph and said, "Come to bed with me!" But he refused. "With me in charge," he told her, "my master does not concern himself with anything in the house; everything he owns he has entrusted to my care. No one is greater in this house than I am. My master has withheld nothing from me except you because you are his wife. How then could I do such a wicked thing and sin against God?" And though she spoke to Joseph day after day, he refused to go to bed with her or even be with her. - Genesis 39:6 - 10 (NIV)

One day he went into the house to attend to his duties, and none of the household servants was inside. She caught him by his cloak and said, "Come to bed with me!" But he left his cloak in her hand and ran out of the house.
When she saw he had left his cloak in her hand and had run out of the house, she called her household servants. "Look," she said to them, "this Hebrew has been brought to us to make sport of us! He came in here to sleep with me, but I screamed. When he heard me scream for help, he left his cloak beside me and ran out of the house." She kept his cloak beside her until his master came home. Then she told him this story: "That Hebrew slave you brought us came to me to make sport of me. But as soon as I screamed for help, he left his cloak beside me and ran out of the house." - Genesis 39:11 - 18 (NIV)

When his master heard the story his wife told him, saying, "This is how your slave treated me," he burned with anger. Joseph's master took him and put him in prison, the place where the king's prisoners were confined.

But while Joseph was there in the prison, the Lord was with him; he showed him kindness and granted him favor in the eyes of the prison warden. So the warden put Joseph in charge of all those held in the prison, and he was made responsible for all that was done there. The warden paid no attention to anything under Joseph's care because the Lord was with Joseph and gave him success in whatever he did. - Genesis 39:19 - 23 (NIV)

Day 5

God-Dreamers Never Give Up

"If you can dream it, you can do it. Always remember that this whole thing was started with a dream and a mouse." Walt Disney

Joseph went from the pit to the palace, to prison and then finally he stands as the Prime Minister of Egypt. One would have to admit that Joseph had ample reason to give up, throw in the towel, become a victim and allow his dream to die. I am sure thankful he did not give up halfway; the entire nation of Israel survived because Joseph refused to give up his God-dream. Joseph was afforded an opportunity to stand before Pharaoh and interpret his dream putting Joseph in a powerful position to lead and rule over not only his brothers who sold him but nations.

I remember preparing this sermon for church on dreams and was so very inspired by the life of Walt Disney. Today thousands of people enjoy a place of fun, joy, music, and laughter. It is a place where the oldest person can become a child again and live in a dream world of joy and peace, and this place was birthed out of a dream in the heart of the man Walt Disney. As I read about his life, I discovered that he created this magical place in his mind to escape his strict and disciplinarian father who administered "corrective" beatings as part of his daily life. Like Joseph, Walt Disney also faced many challenges like losing his work because it was not copyrighted, he had to give up his apartment and lived in his office surviving on eating just cold beans. He started with a dream that created something magical, and it lives on today long after he has gone.

Perhaps you have come to a place where you have given up on your dreams, and your life has lost its luster, your passion from when you were younger might have died. I want to encourage you today, "Please don't give up." God has a good plan for your life and though you might have faced setbacks don't let that keep you down. John Barrymore said, "A man is not old until regrets take the place of dreams." Don't let your dream die with you; dare to see your dreams become a reality.

Prayer: *Lord, thank you for showing me that my life is not over and I can see my dreams come through. Today I realize I am not poor because I still have a God-dream. Amen.*

DAILY SCRIPTURES FOR MEDITATION

Joseph said to his brothers, "I am Joseph! Is my father still living?" But his brothers were not able to answer him because they were terrified at his presence.

Then Joseph said to his brothers, "Come close to me." When they had done so, he said, "I am your brother Joseph, the one you sold into Egypt! And now, do not be distressed and do not be angry with yourselves for selling me here, because it was to save lives that God sent me ahead of you. For two years now there has been famine in the land, and for the next five years there will be no plowing and reaping. But God sent me ahead of you to preserve for you a remnant on earth and to save your lives by a great deliverance. -   Genesis 45:3 - 7 (NIV)

Then Joseph brought his father Jacob in and presented him before Pharaoh. After Jacob blessed Pharaoh, Pharaoh asked him, "How old are you?"

And Jacob said to Pharaoh, "The years of my pilgrimage are a hundred and thirty. My years have been few and difficult, and they do not equal the years of the pilgrimage of my fathers." Then Jacob blessed Pharaoh and went out from his presence.

So Joseph settled his father and his brothers in Egypt and gave them property in the best part of the land, the district of Rameses, as Pharaoh directed. Joseph also provided his father and his brothers and all his father's household with food, according to the number of their children. - Genesis 47:7 - 12 (NIV)

And we know that in all things God works for the good of those who love him, who have been called according to his purpose. - Romans 8:28 (NIV)

Reflections

Plan 3

DIVINE SEPARATION

===

When we hear the word "separation" immediately our thoughts go to a married couple going their separate ways. However, do you know that separation extends to family, friends, or anyone dear to you? Are you aware that "separation" can also be a God-thing? In this plan, we would explore the life of Abraham and how Divine Separation had to happen for him to fulfill the plans and purposes that God had in store for him.

Day 1

A Divine Separation Is Ordained By God For A Greater Purpose – A Divine Purpose!

Usually, when we hear the word separation, it brings with it a great sense of loss and heartbreak. I believe no matter what the separation is it will always hurt in the present moment. But I understand that while all separation is difficult and hurtful not all separation is bad and can be beneficial for us eventually. One of the most devastating separations we can face as humans are being separated from God. But I am so thankful for Jesus and the finished work of the cross; that we no longer must live separated from him, I like to say it like this, "*Now I get to live separated unto him.*"

There are several definitions of the word separation, but the one I most like is, "*The place at which a division or parting occurs.*"

Before we came to the saving grace of Jesus, we found ourselves in a distant place. Once Jesus comes into our lives that gap or distance is removed and we have free access to God the father because of the bridge Jesus made for us. While there is such freedom now to access the Father, the enemy still seeks to keep us from him.

The enemy preys on keeping us in bondage so we will always feel separated from God. He loves to play on our emotions because he is so good at manipulation. One area the enemy keeps God's children in bondage is the area of strife.

The definition of strife is, "*Vigorous or bitter conflict, a quarrel, discord, and antagonism or competition and rivalry.*" Often we find ourselves in strife when we refuse to separate from the people with different values, visions, dreams, and purposes in life. Don't get me wrong; I am not saying that we should be clannish and secluded but when we allow the compromising of our values that go against God's Word and Will for our lives; we will find ourselves in trouble. Sometimes God is calling you to a place where he can pour into you, and that means leaving people aside for that time. God called Abraham to a great destiny with promises beyond his imagination. But God was very specific in Abraham moving away from his family to a place where God would do this great work in him. Abraham did not follow the instructions as he should and took his nephew Lot along. Mind you this nephew caused him a lot of trouble. It is vital for us to understand that following God's instructions will always lead to life and not strife.

Food for thought: *Do I need a divine separation in my life and if so what is God's instructions?*

DAILY SCRIPTURES FOR MEDITATION

Now [in Haran] the Lord said to Abram, Go for yourself [for your own advantage] away from your country, from your relatives and your father's house to the land that I will show you. - Genesis 12:1(AMPC)

And I will make of you a great nation, and I will bless you [with abundant increase of favors] and make your name famous and distinguished, and you will be a blessing [dispensing good to others]. And I will bless those who bless you [who confer prosperity or happiness upon you] and curse him who curses or uses insolent language toward you; in you will all the families and kindred of the earth be blessed [and by you, they will bless themselves]. - Genesis 12:2 - 3(AMPC)

So Abram departed, as the Lord had directed him; and Lot [his nephew] went with him. Abram was seventy-five years old when he left Haran.
Abram took Sarai his wife, and Lot his brother's son, and all their possessions that they had gathered, and the persons [servants] that they had acquired in Haran, and they went forth to go to the land of Canaan. When they came to the land of Canaan, - Genesis 12:4 - 5(AMPC)

Day 2

Get Rid Of Strife In Your Life

With a great vision from God Abraham ventured out to see the fulfillment of his promise all the while taking Lot along who was not part of God's instructions. The Bible records a famine in the land that led Abraham and his family to Egypt. Sometimes the call of God doesn't always lead us on a straight, smooth path but in the curves on the journey, we must believe God's promises are true. Over the course of time, the famine was over, and Abraham's wealth increased, and so did Lot's, but the land they occupied was not large enough to contain them both and all they owned. In our lives, we believe if we don't take care of family members, friends or just people close to us we are not "*Christ-like.*" God specifically told Abraham to leave his family, and all that he knew was familiar so God could do something grand and new in his life. The blessings God bestowed upon Abraham were not to prosper him alone it included all the families of the earth. But initiating the journey was one he needed to start alone with God.

When we take it upon ourselves to bring others along when God did not sanction it we open the door wide to strife. The Bible records that quarreling and discord ensued between the workers of Abraham and Lot due to a lack of space. Sometimes, people come to you for help, they might be in a tight spot and need a hand to get stable, nothing is wrong with lending a helping hand, and we should be very inclined to help those we love in need. But for sharing your personal space especially when you have your own family, it's something that should never be a long-term arrangement. Nothing is wrong with protecting your family and your personal space because without a clear picture of your destiny and lack of discernment you can create a situation for strife to exist.

It would seem that while Abraham was journeying to his promise, he would have recognized how serious God's instructions were to do this on his own. Abraham confronted Lot by practically begging him to separate, to go in the other direction and he gave him the option to choose where he wanted to go. Abraham understood strife would hinder the call on his life.

Food for Thought: *Do I have strife in my life?*

DAILY SCRIPTURES FOR MEDITATION

But Lot, who went with Abram, also had flocks and herds and tents.
Now the land was not able to nourish and support them so they could
dwell together, for their possessions were too great for them to live
together.
And there was strife between the herdsmen of Abram's cattle and the
herdsmen of Lot's cattle. And the Canaanite and the Perizzite were
dwelling then in the land [making fodder more difficult to obtain]. -
Genesis 13:5 -6 (AMPC)

So Abram said to Lot, Let there be no strife, I beg of you, between
you and me, or between your herdsmen and my herdsmen, for we
are relatives.
Is not the whole land before you? Separate yourself, I beg of you,
from me. If you take the left hand, then I will go to the right; or if you
choose the right hand, then I will go to the left. - Genesis 13:8 - 9
(AMPC)

And Lot looked and saw that everywhere the Jordan Valley was well
watered. Before the Lord destroyed Sodom and Gomorrah, [it was
all] like the garden of the Lord, like the land of Egypt, as you go to
Zoar.
Then Lot chose for himself all the Jordan Valley and [he] traveled
east. So they separated.
Abram dwelt in the land of Canaan, and Lot dwelt in the cities of the
[Jordan] Valley and moved his tent as far as Sodom and dwelt there.
But the men of Sodom were wicked and exceedingly great sinners
against the Lord. - Genesis 13:10 - 13 (AMPC)

Day 3

Divine Separation Will Bring Clarity Of The Call And Re-establish The Promises

It is incredible how strife can blind us to the call and vision that God has for our lives. As we saw yesterday Abraham was not willing to allow strife to remain in his life; he did not give it time to grow and fester under the guise of trying to help his family. Abraham saw the heart of Lot when he was given the opportunity to choose where he wanted to live. Abraham had a heart after God and wanted to follow the path that God had for him, but Lot's desire was distinctly different, and his choice showed that. We all know the story of Sodom and Gomorrah and the tragic end for that city pair. Just because we are related to someone doesn't always mean we share the same vision and values.

Interestingly enough once the divine separation took place and Abraham confronted the potential strife in his life; suddenly, God shows up to speak with Abraham and reiterate the promises made to him. The cluttering of Abraham space was blinding him from seeing the bigger picture. So often when we don't confront strife as Abraham did, all our time will be consumed with what the person is doing wrong, or how much of your stuff they are using, and a spirit of complaining develops.

When we get so consumed with strife, it will stifle the vision and keep us blind from all of God's blessings. We seem to live in a society that makes confrontation and separation a bad thing. But in the walk of the believer, it is so necessary to confront and separate from anything that would hinder the call of God in our lives. Believe it or not, your separation from a toxic relationship can put you in a position to even save that person. Please don't misunderstand me; I am not talking about separation in marriages because there is marital counseling that could be done to restore your marriage. I am speaking of relationships outside the bond of marriage.

Once we confront strife and separate from the toxic emotions, there will be the restoration of your vision and call. Perhaps you could not pray and effectively meditate due to strife and a lack of peace internally. Today I want you to know God desires to communicate his plan for your life again. Why not let the strife go today.

Food for Thought: *What situations need I confront today? Am I able to focus on God's plan for my life or am I absorbed with toxic emotions?*

DAILY SCRIPTURES FOR MEDITATION

The Lord said to Abram after Lot had left him, Lift up now your eyes and look from the place where you are, northward and southward and eastward and westward;
For all the land which you see, I will give to you and to your posterity forever. - Genesis 13:14 - 15 (AMPC)

And I will make your descendants like the dust of the earth, so that if a man could count the dust of the earth, then could your descendants also be counted.
Arise, walk through the land, the length of it and the breadth of it, for I will give it to you.
Then Abram moved his tent and came and dwelt among the oaks or terebinths of Mamre, which are at Hebron, and built there an altar to the Lord. - Genesis 13:16 - 18 (AMPC)

Day 4

Divine Separation Will Reveal Hidden Plans For The Future

When we make a conscious and deliberate choice not to allow strife to perpetuate in our lives, it not only gives us clarity of the vision for our own lives but it causes God to share his plans even for the future of others. I had many situations where I kept holding on to people and keeping them in my life even when there were outward signs we did not have the same shared vision and values. One thing that can perpetuate strife is to be in control of others, thinking we know what is best for them and trying to make them go in our direction when their heart is elsewhere. I am not ashamed to say I have suffered from this "control freak" syndrome. I guess because I grew up with little parental guidance and many failures; that I was bent on making sure the people in my life would have a path to follow that was right in my eyes. I had so much strife in my life I was devastated when the actual separation happened.

The reason I can write on this is because I lived in it for many years and due to cultivating strife in my life I was blinded by this notion that to help someone I love I had to keep them close and in my space even if it made me miserable. Somehow I convinced myself I was," suffering for the cause." What a lie from hell! Over the years I have learned that divine separation can give me more clarity in helping the person rather than staying in strife. After Abraham separated from Lot, he developed such a close relationship with God that was so intimate; God was not willing to keep secrets from him. Who would have thought refusing to keep strife in our lives could open our hearts to the plans of God for the future of others. Just Amazing!!!

God was about to investigate the situation in Sodom and Gomorrah and shared his intentions with Abraham because God considered him a friend. I am overwhelmed with the grace of our God toward us who desire to walk in his ways but even to our family and friends in caring to share what might happen if we don't pray for them. If you want to help your loved ones, it is time to clear the clutter so you can be useful for their survival.

Food for Thought: *Am I able to hear what is on God's heart? Do I know what will be the outcome for my loved ones and friends?*

DAILY SCRIPTURES FOR MEDITATION

The men rose up from there and faced toward Sodom, and Abraham went with them to bring them on the way.
And the Lord said, Shall I hide from Abraham [My friend and servant] what I am going to do, - Genesis 18:16 - 17 (AMPC)

Since Abraham shall surely become a great and mighty nation, and all the nations of the earth shall be blessed through him and shall bless themselves by him?
For I have known (chosen, acknowledged) him [as My own], so that he may teach and command his children and the sons of his house after him to keep the way of the Lord and to do what is just and righteous, so that the Lord may bring Abraham what He has promised him. - Genesis 18:18 - 19 (AMPC)

And the Lord said Because the shriek [of the sins] of Sodom and Gomorrah is great and their sin is exceedingly grievous,
I will go down now and see whether they have done altogether [as vilely and wickedly] as is the cry of it which has come to Me; and if not, I will know.
Now the [two] men turned from there and went toward Sodom, but Abraham still stood before the Lord. - Genesis 18:20 - 22 (AMPC)

Day 5

Divine Separation Will Produce Effective Intercession

If we dug deep into the heart of the matter when it comes down to it; the truth is we all have love for our families and friends. At the core of us when we help them it is because we start off genuinely wanting to make a difference, but the misconception is to believe we can change them or cause them to fit into our mold of life. God didn't design their change to take place in that manner because the truth is we will take all the credit for their change. Only God can change the heart of a person, all we can do is love them while still maintaining space and avoiding clutter.

After God shared his plans for Sodom and Gomorrah with Abraham, we get to see a glimpse of what is in Abraham's heart for his nephew Lot. We see Abraham take the opportunity to pray for the city of Sodom and Gomorrah without uttering one mention of Lots name. I love he had such a beautiful relationship with God that even if he did not come outright to say his nephew's name God knew his heart toward him. And God entertains Abraham requests to petition for a city beyond repair. His love for his nephew rose to the surface even though he knew Lot had chosen a life outside of God and had made many poor choices.

Abraham petitioned God for the city based on fifty people being found righteous. I am sure Abraham knew the condition of Sodom and Gomorrah, but in his love for his nephew he was not willing to let him die without trying, and Abraham continued his petitions forty-five, thirty, twenty and then ten righteous people. His heart for Lot was evident, and this was possible because when the time to separate came, he did. Had Abraham not separated from Lot he could never intercede for him.

The city of Sodom and Gomorrah was not saved, but Abraham's intercession saved Lot and his daughters. Today I present to you; the ones you are trying to save in your own strength will only lead you to strife. But if like Abraham you would learn to refuse strife in your life God will use the divine separation to save them.

Food For Thought: *Am I interceding for the people I care about or Am I still trying to save them myself?*

DAILY SCRIPTURES FOR MEDITATION

And Abraham came close and said, Will You destroy the righteous (those upright and in right standing with God) together with the wicked?

Suppose there are in the city fifty righteous; will You destroy the place and not spare it for [the sake of] the fifty righteous in it?

Far be it from You to do such a thing—to slay the righteous with the wicked, so that the righteous fare as do the wicked! Far be it from You! Shall not the Judge of all the earth execute judgment and do righteously?

And the Lord said, If I find in the city of Sodom fifty righteous (upright and in right standing with God), I will spare the whole place for their sake. - Genesis 18:23 - 26 (AMPC)

Abraham answered, Behold now, I who am but dust and ashes have taken upon myself to speak to the Lord.

If five of the fifty righteous should be lacking—will You destroy the whole city for lack of five? He said, If I find forty-five, I will not destroy it.

And [Abraham] spoke to Him yet again, and said, Suppose [only] forty shall be found there. And He said I will not do it for forty's sake.

Then [Abraham] said to Him, Oh, let not the Lord be angry, and I will speak [again]. Suppose [only] thirty shall be found there. And He answered I will not do it if I find thirty there. - Genesis 18:27 - 30 (AMPC)

And [Abraham] said, Behold now, I have taken upon myself to speak [again] to the Lord. Suppose [only] twenty shall be found there. And [the Lord] replied, I will not destroy it for twenty's sake.

And he said, Oh, let not the Lord be angry, and I will speak again only this once. Suppose ten [righteous people] shall be found there. And [the Lord] said, I will not destroy it for ten's sake.

And the Lord went His way when He had finished speaking with Abraham, and Abraham returned to his place. - Genesis 18:31 - 33 (AMPC)

Abraham went up early the next morning to the place where he [only the day before] had stood before the Lord.

And he looked toward Sodom and Gomorrah, and toward all the land of the valley, and saw, and behold, the smoke of the country went up like the smoke of a furnace.

When God ravaged and destroyed the cities of the plain [of Siddim], He [earnestly] remembered Abraham [imprinted and fixed him indelibly on His mind], and He sent Lot out of the midst of the overthrow when He overthrew the cities where Lot lived. - Genesis 19:27 - 29 (AMPC)

Reflections

Plan 4

DON'T LOOK BACK

===

The past holds a river of memories for each of us, some good and bad. The sad thing is many of us continue to look back to the past, which is preventing us from walking into the future that God designed and prepared for us before time began. As you read through this plan, my prayer is that you will release the hold on your past and embrace the future God has for you.

Day 1

A New Start

Doesn't a new start sound great? When life becomes difficult, you have failed several times, you have messed up a perfect relationship, and you are bored of your job, your house, your friends, and family; a new start sounds exciting when we find ourselves stuck in the mediocrities of life. Do you know what Jesus did on the cross over two thousand years ago enables you to have a new start even now? Though many believers know this truth, they still live beneath this truth every day because somehow the lie of the old life seems to envelop their souls. The fact is the enemy of our souls knows if he can keep us looking back we would make little progress in the future God has for us.

We all have a past, and for some, it may be memorable, for others it may be horrible. Whatever the past looks like the enemy majors in causing us to indulge in what was. We serve a God that loves to plan ahead for his children, and scripture tells us that his plans are always good in the end (Jeremiah 29:11NIV). As a pastor, I am afforded the opportunity to minister to many people from the young to old, mature and immature, strong and weak but what I recognize is from the least to the greatest the most common issues among them all is letting go of the past.

I spent or should I say "Wasted" a lot of time and energy on what was, and what could have been. But I am grateful for the present and the bright future that God has for me and you too. I want to encourage you to take your time through this plan and to commit to stop looking back on the negatives in your life. Our memory is not the enemy, but the way we use our memory will determine the detriment. When I look back on life, it is for only moments of seeing what God did and how he has brought me through. As you journey with me, I want you to understand that a new start is available to you no matter where you've been or what you have done. Jesus died to save and give you a brand new start. Jesus specializes in new beginnings, and now I look at every disappointment, hurt and pain as an opportunity to birth something new. We do ourselves a great injustice, and we lock God out when we keep looking back negatively. We were made to move forward, and it's time to stop looking back.

Holy Spirit, help me from today to live my life with a view of what is ahead; help me to stop looking back!

DAILY SCRIPTURES FOR MEDITATION

As for you, you were dead in your transgressions and sins, in which you used to live when you followed the ways of this world and of the ruler of the kingdom of the air, the spirit now at work in those who are disobedient. All of us also lived among them at one time, gratifying the cravings of our flesh and following its desires and thoughts. Like the rest, we were by nature deserving of wrath. But because of his great love for us, God, who is rich in mercy, made us alive with Christ even when we were dead in transgressions—it is by grace you have been saved. - Ephesians 2:1-5 (NIV)

Therefore, if anyone is in Christ, the new creation has come: The old has gone, the new is here! - 2 Corinthians 5:17 (NIV)

Brothers and sisters, I do not consider myself yet to have taken hold of it. But one thing I do: Forgetting what is behind and straining toward what is ahead, I press on toward the goal to win the prize for which God has called me heavenward in Christ Jesus. - Philippians 3:13-14 (NIV)

Day 2

Looking Back Is A Heart Condition

The scriptures teach us that as a man thinks in his heart so is he (Proverbs 23:7 NIV).

If we examined this closer, we could see that most of what we act out in life find its origins in our thoughts. Day after day whatever we ponder on, meditate on and dwell on becomes a reality sooner or later. Our thoughts are powerful and will eventually determine the future we will experience. Have you ever heard the saying "Follow your heart?" Well, there is so much truth wrapped up in that saying, and even the Bible talks about our heart following our treasure (Luke 12:34).

Our heart was made to follow the ultimate treasure which is God himself, but only Jesus could give us the heart to understand that, and without this understanding, we will chase riches of this world of lesser value.

Looking back and living in the past constantly is a clear indication you believe your treasures are still buried there. A woman in the Bible only went by the title of Lots wife, and her heart was so caught up in the treasures of this world she could not see the grand future God had planned out for her. I am sure many of you have heard of the cities of Sodom and Gomorrah and the destruction of fire and brimstone that rained down and ruined them. Lot's wife lived there with her family, and though it was a place of much immorality and disgraces, her heart was very much tied to it. But because of the prayers of Abraham God would save Lot and his family from the devastation. God allowed them enough time to escape with this instruction,

"Do not look behind you nor stay anywhere in the plain." (Genesis 19:17 NIV).

When I look back at my life, I am so thankful that God brought me out of many situations that would have only resulted in my destruction had I stayed there. In the moment of having to leave behind people, possessions and relationships we hold close and dear to us may seem like the most challenging thing to do. But when you put your trust in the One who knows best; the present pain will eventually turn into the greatest gain in life. Lot's wife's treasures were so buried in the city she had to leave behind that she was not willing to trust God with the future. The Bible tells us that as she was leaving the city she "Looked back" and was turned into a pillar of salt. The truth about looking back constantly and living in the past is that it will drain the very life from you. Let us heed the warning of God and make sure our heart is following him.

Holy Spirit, help me today to leave the past behind and lead me to an abundant life ahead!

DAILY SCRIPTURES FOR MEDITATION

For where your treasure is, there your heart will be also. - Luke 12:34(NIV)

With the coming of dawn, the angels urged Lot, saying, "Hurry! Take your wife and your two daughters who are here, or you will be swept away when the city is punished."
When he hesitated, the men grasped his hand and the hands of his wife and of his two daughters and led them safely out of the city, for the Lord was merciful to them. As soon as they had brought them out, one of them said, "Flee for your lives! Don't look back, and don't stop anywhere in the plain! Flee to the mountains or you will be swept away!" - Genesis 19:15 - 17 (NIV)

But Lot said to them, "No, my lords, please! Your servant has found favor in your eyes, and you have shown great kindness to me in sparing my life. But I can't flee to the mountains; this disaster will overtake me, and I'll die. Look, here is a town near enough to run to, and it is small. Let me flee to it—it is very small, isn't it? Then my life will be spared."
He said to him, "Very well, I will grant this request too; I will not overthrow the town you speak of. But flee there quickly, because I cannot do anything until you reach it." (That is why the town was called Zoar.) - Genesis 19:18 - 22 (NIV)

By the time Lot reached Zoar, the sun had risen over the land. Then the Lord rained down burning sulfur on Sodom and Gomorrah—from the Lord out of the heavens. Thus he overthrew those cities and the entire plain, destroying all those living in the cities—and also the vegetation in the land. But Lot's wife looked back, and she became a pillar of salt. - Genesis 19:23 - 26 (NIV)

Brothers and sisters, I do not consider myself yet to have taken hold of it. But one thing I do: Forgetting what is behind and straining toward what is ahead, I press on toward the goal to win the prize for which God has called me heavenward in Christ Jesus. - Philippians 3:13-14 (NIV)

Day 3

Looking Back Feeds The Desires Of The Flesh Providing A False Sense Of Security

When we look back and constantly dwell on the past, it seems to offer us a sense of safety even if the situation we were in was a dangerous one physically, emotionally or mentally. This is because as humans, change and newness always bring with it a sense of challenge, stretching and the unknown. But in the past we find comfort because we know all that we were dealing with, it was familiar even though it was difficult. Sounds strange, I know but I have seen time and time again in ministry where people will go back to abusive homes, manipulative relationships and immoral lifestyles just because it's familiar and provides a false sense of security.

I grew up in an abusive home, and it seemed easier to deal with the abuse than to open up to someone in authority for help; again it was the unknown of the future that kept me bound to that situation. Today I am writing about moving from the past and looking forward to the future because the life that God has for his children is always better than what we will leave behind. The children of Israel did not differ from us today, even though they were slaves in Egypt and cried out to God for freedom and help, they never seemed to let go of the past and the bondage that felt familiar to them. Their lives were plagued with beatings and hard labor from their taskmasters. The Hebrew men were belittled and disrespected in front of their wives and children, and they cried out to God. We are told in scriptures that God heard their cries and remembered his covenant with their forefathers and sent a deliverer - Moses to bring them out of Egypt.

I find comfort and encouragement from this story of the Exodus while it may have ended tragically for many; it serves as wisdom to us who study their lives to learn from their mistakes. Often we cry out to God to save us from our situations, but truthfully we want the saving on our terms and not his which breeds disappointments, and that causes us to look back. If only we could come to place in our lives where we believe God's plan is better than ours. The Israelites wanted to come out of bondage, but they did not trust God, and they longed to go back to Egypt for the false sense of security it provided to them. They did not see the wilderness as temporary or that God was with them in the coming out; all they could think about was what they had when they were in bondage.

Holy Spirit, help me today to let go of the familiar and the false sense of security of the past. Please help me to trust you with this process.

DAILY SCRIPTURES FOR MEDITATION

Then the Lord said to Moses, "Tell the Israelites to turn back and encamp near Pi Hahiroth, between Migdol and the sea. They are to encamp by the sea, directly opposite Baal Zephon. Pharaoh will think, 'The Israelites are wandering around the land in confusion, hemmed in by the desert.' And I will harden Pharaoh's heart, and he will pursue them. But I will gain glory for myself through Pharaoh and all his army, and the Egyptians will know that I am the Lord. "So the Israelites did this. - Exodus 14:1 - 4 (NIV)

As Pharaoh approached, the Israelites looked up, and there were the Egyptians, marching after them. They were terrified and cried out to the Lord. They said to Moses, "Was it because there were no graves in Egypt that you brought us to the desert to die? What have you done to us by bringing us out of Egypt? Didn't we say to you in Egypt, 'Leave us alone; let us serve the Egyptians'? It would have been better for us to serve the Egyptians than to die in the desert!" - Exodus 14:10 - 11 (NIV)

Brothers and sisters, I do not consider myself yet to have taken hold of it. But one thing I do: Forgetting what is behind and straining toward what is ahead, I press on toward the goal to win the prize for which God has called me heavenward in Christ Jesus. - Philippians 3:13-14 (NIV)

Day 4

Looking Back Feeds The Desires Of The Flesh - A Longing For Supplies

As we go further into the story of the children of Israel in the wilderness, we can see how much their heart was rooted in the bondage of Egypt. It is incredible how much food plays a huge part in any culture. In New York, one highlight of the city is the many restaurants and the diversity of culinary cuisines. Food can comfort us on a cold night, it is the highlight of every party and what has always puzzled me is going to the theater to see your favorite movie yet that experience is never complete without something to munch on. I guess what I'm trying to say is that food seems to infiltrate most aspects of our lives and Jesus was acutely aware of the tendency to lean on food as a substitute for God. In one of the recorded temptations of Jesus in his wilderness experience, the devil challenged him to turn the stone into bread, and Jesus response was, "It is written: man shall not live by bread alone but by every word that comes from the mouth of God." (Matthew 4:4 NIV)

I know you might be wondering what food must do with looking back. Well, let us look at what happened to the children of Israel. After they left Egypt; they crossed the red sea and started their journey in the wilderness, God was with them through it all. God was their shade and cool in the daytime in a cloud, and He was their warmth and protector by night in a pillar of fire. God moved with them, and He became their source, but their flesh was so attached to Egypt for the supplies they had in abundance they could not see the many provisions in the present by the very hand of God. This looking back mentality caused them to grumble and complain rather than be thankful. It is a dangerous thing to live desiring for what was and making light of what is. Many good relationships end when a partner cannot let go of the past. While this reference is about the food there is other material stuff and connivances we can keep looking back for.

Perhaps you were in an abusive relationship, but your partner would overcompensate in material supplies to keep you in bondage, and now that you are out of the abuse your heart still longs for the stuff. Perhaps you complain about the provisions you have now even though the situation is far safer for you. I want to encourage you to keep your eyes on the Lord as he leads you through the process of detoxing your soul of the past. The Bible tells us that the past was so deeply rooted in the hearts of the Israelites they lusted for the supplies of Egypt. (Numbers 11:4 – 6 AMP). God wants to set you free from the bondage of the past. Won't you take his help today?

Holy Spirit, help me to let go of the lust of fleshly things in my past and help me to have an attitude of gratitude for all that you provide me with daily.

DAILY SCRIPTURES FOR MEDITATION

In the desert, the whole community grumbled against Moses and Aaron. The Israelites said to them, "If only we had died by the Lord's hand in Egypt! There we sat around pots of meat and ate all the food we wanted, but you have brought us out into this desert to starve this entire assembly to death." - Exodus 16:2-3 (NIV)

But the people were thirsty for water there, and they grumbled against Moses. They said, "Why did you bring us up out of Egypt to make us and our children and livestock die of thirst?" - Exodus 17:3 (NIV)

The rabble with them began to crave other food, and again the Israelites started wailing and said, "If only we had meat to eat! We remember the fish we ate in Egypt at no cost—also the cucumbers, melons, leeks, onions, and garlic. But now we have lost our appetite; we never see anything but this manna!" - Numbers 11:4-6 (NIV)

Jesus answered, "It is written: 'Man shall not live by bread alone, but on every word that comes from the mouth of God.'" - Matthew 4:4 (NIV)

Brothers and sisters, I do not consider myself yet to have taken hold of it. But one thing I do: Forgetting what is behind and straining toward what is ahead, I press on toward the goal to win the prize for which God has called me heavenward in Christ Jesus. -   Philippians 3:13-14 (NIV)

Day 5

Looking Back Limits The Future

It is heartbreaking to see so many people live their lives camping out in the past that cannot be changed and turning their backs on a grand future. We all know it is impossible to be effective in two places simultaneously and the only person who could accomplish that is God. We can never give one hundred percent of ourselves in the present if we keep dwelling on the past. Our potential will never reach its maximum capacity; future goals get delayed, insecurity and fear will dominate, the flesh will rule and life will become one heap of complaining. There is a lot at stake to remain, and truthfully your life will be unhappy.

The children of Israel found themselves in extreme bondage, they cried to God to deliver them, and God sent a deliverer. They experienced firsthand the goodness, kindness, protection, and provision of God. He split the Red Sea, he destroyed their enemies, he made bitter water sweet, he rained manna from heaven and fed them, their shoes never wore out, and their clothes were kept. He covered them, moved with them, and most of all loved them even when they complained. But they could not let go of the past and that blinded them to the glorious future God had for them. They were eyewitnesses to the Promised Land flowing with milk and honey but because they did not rid themselves of the "Look back mentality" they saw the giants in the land rather than the big, big God with them. The past kept them in fear, and they doubted God's plans. Because of their evil report of the goodness of God; they never made it to the promise land.

Today the stories told in this plan is of greater value than silver and gold. It may have been too late for the Israelites in the wilderness, but it's not too late for you. Living in the past is of great detriment to your future. I want to ask you today to leave the past behind, clear your heart of the clutter and take hold of the glorious future God has planned out for you. The past is over; God is about moving forward!

Holy Spirit, I thank you for the revelation I received, and I genuinely want to make it into the future God has for me. I am sorry I've wasted so much time on the things I cannot change, I am sorry for taking for granted what you so freely provide for me every day. I am sorry for robbing the people in my life because of the "look back mentality."

Holy Spirit, help me to forget the pain associated with the past and as I visit my past from now on let it be for only moments of remembering how you brought me out of bondage. Thank you, Abba for a new start!

DAILY SCRIPTURES FOR MEDITATION

So they went up and explored the land from the Desert of Zin as far as Rehob, toward Lebo Hamath. They went up through the Negev and came to Hebron, where Ahiman, Sheshai and Talmai, the descendants of Anak, lived. (Hebron had been built seven years before Zoan in Egypt.) When they reached the Valley of Eshkol, they cut off a branch bearing a single cluster of grapes. Two of them carried it on a pole between them, along with some pomegranates and figs. That place was called the Valley of Eshkol because of the cluster of grapes the Israelites cut off there. At the end of forty days, they returned from exploring the land. - Numbers 13:21 - 25 (NIV)

They came back to Moses and Aaron and the whole Israelite community at Kadesh in the Desert of Paran. There they reported to them and to the whole assembly and showed them the fruit of the land. They gave Moses this account: "We went into the land to which you sent us, and it does flow with milk and honey! Here is its fruit. But the people who live there are powerful and the cities are fortified and very large. We even saw descendants of Anak there. The Amalekites live in the Negev; the Hittites, Jebusites, and Amorites live in the hill country; and the Canaanites live near the sea and along the Jordan." - Numbers 13:26 - 29 (NIV)

Then Caleb silenced the people before Moses and said, "We should go up and take possession of the land, for we can certainly do it." But the men who had gone up with him said, "We can't attack those people; they are stronger than we are." And they spread among the Israelites a bad report about the land they had explored. They said, "The land we explored devours those living in it. All the people we saw there are of great size. We saw the Nephilim there (the descendants of Anak come from the Nephilim). We seemed like grasshoppers in our own eyes, and we looked the same to them." - Numbers 13:30 - 33 (NIV)

The Lord replied, "I have forgiven them, as you asked. Nevertheless, as surely as I live and as surely as the glory of the Lord fills the whole earth, not one of those who saw my glory and the signs I performed in Egypt and in the wilderness but who disobeyed me and tested me ten times— not one of them will ever see the land I promised on oath to their ancestors. No one who has treated me with contempt will ever see it. - Numbers 14:20 - 23 (NIV)

For I know the plans I have for you," declares the Lord, "plans to prosper you and not to harm you, plans to give you hope and a future. - Jeremiah 29:11(NIV)

Brothers and sisters, I do not consider myself yet to have taken hold of it. But one thing I do: Forgetting what is behind and straining toward what is ahead, I press on toward the goal to win the prize for which God has called me heavenward in Christ Jesus. - Philippians 3:13-14 (NIV)

Reflections

_____
_____
_____
_____
_____
_____
_____
_____
_____
_____
_____
_____
_____
_____
_____
_____
_____
_____
_____
_____
_____
_____
_____
_____
_____

Plan 5

FAITH VS FATE

==

In the world, many people view their destiny as their *Fate*- or as the saying goes, *"whatever will be, will be."* But as a believer, *Faith* is the word that should be part of our vocabulary, for *faith* is a gift given to men after they have put their trust in God and this *faith* can chart a different course for your life. Are you *fate-driven* or are you *faith-driven*? I hope this plan will help you move from a fate to faith mindset!

Day 1

Fate

When God created the human race, he created them in his image and likeness according to the book of Genesis in the Bible. Man was created in the likeness of his Creator, and God has written a good plan for our lives, but God does not dictate or demand we take his way because he created us with the power to choose. The ability to choose is what sets us apart from all other creations, and that is a lot of power we have been given when you think about it. God had perfection in mind for us when he created mankind, but our first earthly father and mother - Adam and Eve, chose against God's best for them and perfection were tainted. But then, God the Father sent his son Jesus, the second Adam, to give us a second chance at choosing God's best, but today many people are still taking the path of the first Adam which will only lead to death.

I hear the saying all the time from people who have not chosen Jesus as their Lord, "Whatever will be, will be." Have you ever heard that statement also? If we look deeper into that statement, it is bone-chilling to think that whatever happens in life was meant to be, but unfortunately, that is the modus operandi of the world. But I beg to differ that if this belief system is true, then what is the reason for prayer, quiet times with the Lord, fasting, or even going to church? If our lives were lived with this predestined path of unfortunate and tragic events with a few happy moments between, then why would Jesus even need to come to earth to save us?

There are two beliefs system that many people live by in the world and one is *fate* and the other is *faith*. Fate is the will or principle or determining cause by which things, in general, are believed to come to be as they are or events to happen as they do. Fate is also defined as something that unavoidably befalls a person or that which is inevitably predetermined: destiny. With this definition, it gives the idea that if someone has a beautiful end to their destiny, it will happen to them no matter what and nothing they do can change it. This sounds great, but on the flip side, if someone has a bad end to their destiny there is also nothing they can do to change it. This belief system sounds very flawed and very unfair. But it also shows that the author of our destiny seems to have biases, and this is not the God who created man in his image.

If Jesus gave his life for us in the extent of such bitter and physical abuse even unto death to return us to the position of right standing with our Heavenly Father, then the belief system of "Whatever will be, will be" should have no space in our lives. When Jesus died and rose again from the dead, our Heavenly Father not only gave us eternal life, but He blessed us with every spiritual blessing in Christ – "Praise be to the God and Father of our Lord Jesus Christ, who has blessed us in the heavenly realms with every spiritual blessing in Christ" (Ephesians 1:3 NIV). This suggests that though our destiny was derailed by Adam's wrong choice now because of the position of Jesus, He has reestablished us to our destiny which can now be changed to the perfect plan God has for us and it is no longer, "Whatever will be, will be"!

> *"I've seen dreams that move the mountains, hope that doesn't ever end, even when the sky is falling. I've seen miracles just happen, silent prayers get answered, broken hearts become brand new — That's what faith can do"* ~ Kutless.

DAILY SCRIPTURES FOR MEDITATION

So God created mankind in his own image,in the image of God he created them; male and female he created them. - Genesis 1:27 (NIV)

For I know the plans I have for you," declares the Lord, "plans to prosper you and not to harm you, plans to give you hope and a future. - Jeremiah 29:11 (NIV)

For just as through the disobedience of the one man the many were made sinners, so also through the obedience of the one man the many will be made righteous. - Romans 5:19 (NIV)

Day 2

Faith

Today we want to focus on the other belief system, and most believers live their lives by it - that is *faith*. The Greek word for faith according to Strong's concordance is *pistis*, and it means "*Firm persuasion*" – a conviction based upon hearing. Strong also notes, "Faith (4102/pistis) is always a gift from God, and never something that can be produced by people. In short, 4102/pistis ("faith") for the believer is "*God's divine persuasion*" – and therefore distinct from human belief (confidence), yet involving it. The Lord continuously births faith in the yielded believer so they can know what he prefers, i.e., *the persuasion of His will*" – "for everyone born of God overcomes the world. This is the victory that has overcome the world, even our faith" (1 John 5:4 NIV).

From the definition above we can see that faith is a gift given to men after they have put their trust in him, and this faith isn't just given as a one-time gift but rather a continuous, growing, and progressive gift. I want you to pay close attention to the statement in the definition, "*A conviction based on hearing.*" That is the way we get faith, the Bible tells us, "So then faith comes by hearing, and hearing by the word of God." (Romans 10:17 NKJV). True faith can only come by continuously hearing the words of Christ, the good news and the promises of God. The enemy of our souls (Satan) would love to engraft the erroneous belief of, "Whatever will be, will be," but God's words are true and powerful and can chart a very different course for our lives even if we were previously heading for doom.

I am so grateful for the gift of faith because it changed my life, and I am praying it would change yours also. For many years I believed in fate, I believed my life was destined for doom and gloom, I believed I was useless because of the color of my skin and the texture of my hair, because of my lack of money, and educational background. I believed these lies because I always heard words of rejection, and the enemy magnified those words, and I was ready for living a life of failure. Perhaps you are in a place where you are also listening to the lies of the enemy about your destiny. Perhaps the enemy has convinced you because of the alcoholic history, or violent and abusive traits of your father you will also be like him, or maybe you come from deep poverty and have no education, or your family line is plagued with divorce and heartbreak and you believe you are heading down the same path.

I don't know what your plight might be, but the God who created you does, and if he spoke to you right now he would say, "Son or Daughter, I know your genealogy, history, and present, but I have always had a good plan for you, would you trust me in this moment and forget all the lies you've been told? Today I want to give you a gift called faith, and with it, you can chart a different course for your life. It doesn't have to turn out how it did for the generations past, I offered them the gift, but they didn't want it. Come to me, believe me, and I will give you rest."

> *"There is still One whose faith in you has never wavered. And how wonderful it is that that one should be Jesus Christ! It was a wonderful dream God dreamed; Christ says when He created you; it was a stately being that was in His mind when you were fashioned, and I can make you all He meant that you should be."* ~ A. J. Gossip

DAILY SCRIPTURES FOR MEDITATION

Now faith is confidence in what we hope for and assurance about what we do not see. - Hebrews 11:1 (NIV)

For by the grace given me I say to every one of you: Do not think of yourself more highly than you ought, but rather think of yourself with sober judgment, in accordance with the faith God has distributed to each of you. - Romans 12:3 (NIV)

"Come to me, all you who are weary and burdened, and I will give you rest." - Matthew 11:28 (NIV)

Day 3

Faith Pleases God

When I ponder the thought of pleasing God, it brings delight to my soul now, but it was not always that way. Because of the many negative teachings, I heard while growing up about God the term "Pleasing God" was anything but delightful I would say more fear was associated with the statement. This stems from my personal experience I had with the lack of a father figure in my life, so it was easy for me to adopt that God was hard to please and that drained my soul. But now, being married to a wonderful man and having two children of my own I have been able to see the love of a father through their eyes; because of this revelation, my relationship with my heavenly father has become delightful.

When we understand God loved us even while we were rebellious to him and there is nothing more we can do to please him for acceptance, we have found faith. The gift of faith shows him how much our confidence is in him. My kids need not please me for me to love them more; my love was fixed from the moment I laid eyes on them, and nothing they do can make me love them less or more.

When our kids do something out of love and appreciation for us, that moves us to magnify our love at that moment where our hearts are pleased. In the same way when we bring praise and thanksgiving, or just valuing time in God's presence pleases his heart also. Pleasing God is not hard and laborious work, but instead, it is the exercising of faith in the One who can do the impossible. The Bible tells us God is a rewarder of those that seek him – "And without faith, it is impossible to please God because anyone who comes to him must believe that he exists and that he rewards those who earnestly seek him." (Hebrews 11:6 NIV). To please God doesn't require our works and ability in ourselves, but pleasing God is resting in who he is and his ability to do what he says he will do, and this faith is only maintained by reading, hearing and meditating on him and his words.

In Hebrews 11, we read about the heroes of faith, and they were all very simple people like you and me but their confidence in God to come through for them is what etched their names in the hall of faith – they pleased God because they believed in him. When we put our trust and confidence in our Creator rather than in creation, we will be positioned to see mountains move; oceans parted, supplies never run dry, dead bones live and death defeated. One hero of faith skipped death completely, and all we know is that he walked faithfully with God and one-day God took him – "Enoch walked faithfully with God; then he was no more because God took him away." (Genesis 5:24 NIV). How beautiful it would be to have our names engraved in the hall of faith in heaven. It's not too late my friends to please God - just come to him, believe who he says he is, and watch him do what he said he would do. Take the step of faith today and trust him!

"Faith looks not at what happens to him but at Him Whom he believes." ~Watchman Nee

DAILY SCRIPTURES FOR MEDITATION

The fundamental fact of existence is that this trust in God, this faith, is the firm foundation under everything that makes life worth living. It's our handle on what we can't see. The act of faith is what distinguished our ancestors, set them above the crowd.

Hebrews 11:1-2 (MSG)

Day 4

Prompted By Faith

Faith is progressive. As we grow in our walk with God, and as we become more aware of his presence, and his promises we are able to believe him for greater things. When I started my walk with God, I had little faith, and I would pray for things for myself and my family. I would ask for personal material needs, but I did not believe God wanted to heal my headache as much as he wanted to provide for me so I would suffer physical pain because I didn't yet understand God could heal. As years went by and I studied God's word, it opened up a vault of treasures hidden in plain sight, and my mind understood the depth of love my Father had for me. My faith grew, and then I believed God could heal me just like he healed so many in the Bible. Now I can say I have moved out of the small sphere into a broader realm of faith, and I know I still have a long way to go, but now I can believe God for nations, mass deliverance, and healings all because I increased my time I spent with God and meditating on his word.

In Hebrews 11 we also hear about the great man Moses, his life was extraordinary, and he lived a life of faith in God. But before Moses' life went into depth, there is a small mention of his parents. Moses parents were slaves in Egypt, and they lived in terrifying times; Pharaoh passed a law that all baby boys born in that time should be thrown in the river Nile, but the girls could live. Pharaoh was afraid the Hebrew people would overpower him and his people. But Moses's parents refused to kill him, and they hid him for three months because they believed God could save him. The Amplified Bible says it this way, "[Prompted] by faith Moses, after his birth, was kept concealed for three months by his parents, because they saw how comely the child was; and they were not overawed and terrified by the king's decree." (Hebrews 11:23 AMPC)

The parents of Moses were from the tribe of Levi, the priestly tribe, and they were very familiar with the promise made to Abraham they would one day have their own land and be a free people, and because of the promises of God to their ancestors, they never lost hope or their faith. They trusted God to keep Moses, and God honored their faith in him to do it. Moses' parents took a great leap of faith, and Moses ended up living like royalty in Pharaoh's palace and was still raised by His natural mother, all because his parents were prompted by faith in their God. Maybe today you are facing a detrimental situation with nowhere to turn, and you feel hopeless, I want to encourage you today like Moses' parents to spend time in God's presence reading his promises and let him prompt you for the next move in your life, let go of your situations and let God take control because he has a plan!

"Faith is the willingness to risk anything on God." ~ Jack Hyles

DAILY SCRIPTURES FOR MEDITATION

The fundamental fact of existence is that this trust in God, this faith, is the firm foundation under everything that makes life worth living. It's our handle on what we can't see. The act of faith is what distinguished our ancestors, set them above the crowd. - Hebrews 11:1-2 (MSG)

Then Pharaoh gave this order to all his people: "Every Hebrew boy that is born you must throw into the Nile, but let every girl live." - Exodus 1:22 (NIV)

Now a man of the tribe of Levi married a Levite woman, and she became pregnant and gave birth to a son. When she saw that he was a fine child, she hid him for three months. But when she could hide him no longer, she got a papyrus basket for him and coated it with tar and pitch. Then she placed the child in it and put it among the reeds along the bank of the Nile. His sister stood at a distance to see what would happen to him.
Then Pharaoh's daughter went down to the Nile to bathe, and her attendants were walking along the riverbank. She saw the basket among the reeds and sent her female slave to get it. She opened it and saw the baby. He was crying, and she felt sorry for him. "This is one of the Hebrew babies," she said.
Then his sister asked Pharaoh's daughter, "Shall I go and get one of the Hebrew women to nurse the baby for you?"
"Yes, go," she answered. So the girl went and got the baby's mother. Pharaoh's daughter said to her, "Take this baby and nurse him for me,

and I will pay you." So the woman took the baby and nursed him. When the child grew older, she took him to Pharaoh's daughter, and he became her son. She named him Moses, saying, "I drew him out the water." - Exodus 2:10 (NIV)

Day 5

Four Stages In Progressive Faith

Moses' story is always one of amazement, and his parent's faith is what preserved his life so that he would one day become the deliverer of the people of Israel. I wonder what would have happened if Moses' mother accepted the fate presented to her. I am sure God could have raised up another person, but before the foundation of the earth God had written the plan for Moses' life, and he would look for partners of faith to bring his plan to fruition. I am sure glad Moses' parents didn't sit on the bank of the river Nile and said, "Whatever will be, will be."

Today as we come to a close I want us to examine the scriptures in Hebrews 11 about Moses and pay attention to the words used in the Amplified Bible as the author describes Moses' journey.

1. Aroused faith

When our faith is aroused we can:

Conquer the things of the world and refuse to be called a son of bondage -   (Moses refused to be called the son of Pharaoh's daughter).

We can take up the greater cause for Christ, and his church even if it means being cut off from being popular according to the world standards – (Moses preferred to share in the oppression of his own people).

We can weigh our choices and make Godly decisions – (Moses gave up the riches and comfort in bondage to have freedom with God).

[Aroused] by faith Moses, when he had grown to maturity and become great, refused to be called the son of Pharaoh's daughter,

Because he preferred to share the oppression [suffer the hardships] and bear the shame of the people of God rather than to have the fleeting enjoyment of a sinful life.

He considered the contempt and abuse and shame [borne for] the Christ (the Messiah Who was to come) to be greater wealth than all the treasures of Egypt, for he looked forward and away to the reward (recompense). Hebrews 11:24-26 (AMPC)

2. Motivated faith

When our faith is motivated we can:

Conquer fears of the present situations and circumstances and look to the One who promises – (Moses left Egypt).

[Motivated] by faith he left Egypt behind him, being unawed and undismayed by the wrath of the king; for he never flinched but held staunchly to his purpose and endured steadfastly as one who gazed on him Who is invisible. Hebrews (11:27 AMPC)

3. Simple faith

When we operate in simple faith we can:

Depend on God as your only source of life, needs, protection, health, wholeness, and wealth - (Moses instituted the Passover)

By faith (simple trust and confidence in God) he instituted and carried out the Passover and the sprinkling of the blood [on the doorposts] so that the destroyer of the firstborn (the angel) might not touch those [of the children of Israel]. Hebrews 11:28 (AMPC)

4. Urged on faith

When urged on by faith we can:

Set the stage for miracles - (with God's help Moses parted the Red Sea)

Release everything into God's hands – (Moses had total faith as he led the people of Israel in the dry path of the sea)

See the enemy defeated by the very same thing that was your deliverance – Moses saw the Egyptian army drown in the Red Sea).

[Urged on] by faith the people crossed the Red Sea as [though] on dry land, but when the Egyptians tried to do the same thing they were swallowed up [by the sea]. Hebrews 11:29 (AMPC)

So you see my friends, faith is progressive, but with every level, while there may be more difficult obstacles to overcome, it becomes easier to trust God who is greater than our troubles. Faith catches God's attention because faith screams, "I can't do this Lord but I know you can!" Without fail, God will show up at every juncture of faith. I pray that you will live your life by faith and not fate.

"Faith never knows where it is being led, but it loves and knows the One who is leading." ~ Oswald Chambers

DAILY SCRIPTURES FOR MEDITATION

The fundamental fact of existence is that this trust in God, this faith, is the firm foundation under everything that makes life worth living. It's our handle on what we can't see. The act of faith is what distinguished our ancestors, set them above the crowd. - Hebrews 11:1-2 (MSG)

Fight the good fight of the faith; lay hold of the eternal life to which you were summoned and [for which] you confessed the good confession [of faith] before many witnesses. - 1 Timothy 6:12 (AMPC)

So let us seize and hold fast and retain without wavering the [a]hope we cherish and confess and our acknowledgment of it, for He Who promised is reliable (sure) and faithful to His word. - Hebrews 10:23 (AMPC)

Reflections

_____

_____

_____

_____

_____

_____

_____

_____

_____

_____

_____

_____

_____

_____

_____

_____

_____

_____

_____

_____

_____

_____

_____

_____

_____

Plan 6

FINISHING STRONG

==

Have you ever wanted something so desperately that despite the hindrances and setbacks you persevered until you had it in your grasp? Well, walking with Jesus is similar. Though the road to the finish line can be long, frustrating, bumpy, and filled with so many ups and downs, you can determine to fashion your life like the Apostle Paul and keep your eyes on the prize, God will give you the strength to keep on going and to finish strong.

Day 1

Count The Cost

"Beginning well is a momentary thing; finishing well is a lifelong thing." - Ravi Zacharias

Starting something new is always exciting. Even though we may have fears initially, but I think in general we all look forward to a new thing. Often I've ventured out into new phases of my life, I could still remember my first day of elementary school; it was scary but exciting all simultaneously. Every idea for a new project, venture, or journey breeds deep excitement in our souls. In life we all love to start; be it dating, marriage, joining the workforce, college, the gym, business, a ministry, a creative project, or a family. Whatever it may be, we all look forward to the beginning of something new because it always sounds and feels magical in our minds. We get a feeling of euphoria which we hope would never disappear. Starting is infused with positives only, and our thoughts may roam the expanse of possibilities, and the results always end well in our minds. Starting is terrific, but there is something more powerful than starting, it is finishing.

Jesus in one of his teachings addressed starting and finishing, and while he was speaking on following him, he used natural examples to reiterate his point - (Luke 14:28 – 37 NIV). Life is full of many great starters, but unfortunately, the numbers dwindle with finishers. When we stop for a moment and look around the world today globally or even in our communities, we can see the effects of the starters that never finished. There are increasing numbers of single-parent homes with mostly absentee fathers, divorce, and teenage pregnancies. There are growing numbers of homeless individuals and families, businesses are closing their doors, and the list can go on and on if we pay close attention to the many unfinished scenarios.

Jesus urged us to count the cost before we start because he knew the giddy feelings we would encounter once we get ideas that sound great to us. He knew we could get so caught up in starting and forget the cost involved to finish our assignments. I have seen and experienced so many heartbreaks and disappointments, so many tears, and sleepless nights all because I didn't count the cost, and I didn't consider the whole picture; creating my own failure. For example, a marriage. It is so easy to start a marriage but often-times we confuse the wedding day with marriage, and when we finally realize the journey of marriage will cost a lot to finish we get disappointed. Many marriages today are in a state of flux because the cost was not counted initially. God works differently from our world system, the Word tells us, "For he chose us in him before the creation of the world to be holy and blameless in his sight. In love, he predestined us for adoption to sonship through Jesus Christ, in accordance with his pleasure and will." (Ephesians 1: 4-5 NIV). God knows the end from the beginning (Isaiah 46:10 NIV), God counted the cost to the end, and then he started creation. So too we must count the cost before we start anything, and calculate a strong finish even before we start.

DAILY SCRIPTURES FOR MEDITATION

"Suppose one of you wants to build a tower. Won't you first sit down and estimate the cost to see if you have enough money to complete it? For if you lay, the foundation and are not able to finish it, everyone who sees it will ridicule you, saying, 'This person began to build and wasn't able to finish.' - Luke 14:28-30 (NIV)

For he chose us in him before the creation of the world to be holy and blameless in his sight. In love, he predestined us for adoption to sonship through Jesus Christ, in accordance with his pleasure and will— to the praise of his glorious grace, which he has freely given us in the One he loves. - Ephesians 1:4-6 (NIV)

I make known the end from the beginning, from ancient times, what is still to come. I say, 'My purpose will stand, and I will do all that I please.' - Isaiah 46:10 (NIV)

Day 2

Jesus Finished Strong

"Do not be lazy. Run each day's race with all your might, so that at the end you will receive the victory wreath from God. Keep on running even when you have had a fall. The victory wreath is won by him who does not stay down, but always gets up again, grasps the banner of faith and keeps on running in the assurance that Jesus is Victor." - Basilea Schlink

Jesus' whole assignment on earth was to finish the work his father sent him to do, and he counted the cost before he took his first step into time. Jesus moved and operated with the end in mind. Every step, every word, every prayer, every miracle, every sermon was done with great resolve to finish. Jesus was motivated to finish because his sole purpose was to do the will of his father, and it was the Father's heart to save us, to have us draw near to him again without the issues of sin, judgment, and condemnation.

Jesus knew the Father's heart for us and kept that ever before him knowing he one day must stare death in its face, be separated from the Father he loved so dearly, and literally become sin for us. Jesus counted the cost even though he knew his journey would be tough. He was talked about, scorned, mocked and ridiculed, misjudged and mistreated, falsely accused, beaten beyond recognition, and literally died of a broken heart in his assignment. If we sit and reason the sacrifice Jesus made for us, we would recognize he had many opportunities to stop short, to give up, and to turn his back on his assignment, but something kept him going and that was the desire to fulfill the desire of his Father's heart to save us.

Jesus' ability to finish his assignment on earth would not only save us, but it served as proof to all humanity that God was real, and he did send Jesus to save us. So too when focused on God's word as food and nourishment for our souls; when we desire above all else to do the Father's will, we will be fueled to finish what we start, and in finishing strong we bear witness to others that God is real. For example, when facing hardships in your marriage, or days when money is running low, and the bills keep mounting, or the business venture is not profitable, or the ministry seems stunted in growth, but you keep holding on the promises of God, you keep smiling, you keep trying with joy and peace; people around you will stop and take notice, and they will give credit to God because of the fruit of you staying your course.

Jesus was nourished by his Father's words, he desired to do the will of the father, but he also had a vision of what he would gain once his assignment was completed which was to be reunited with his father, sitting at his right hand but also gaining us to spend eternity with him with no more fear, no more tears, no more pain and no more death.

Jesus gained physically, emotional and mental strength to run his race to the finish because he kept his eye on the prize. Perhaps today you are caught in the web of having had a great start, but now the trials, obstacles, hardships, and torment is causing you to want to quit and walk away. I want to encourage you to keep your eyes on the prize and the end product. Keep your eyes on Jesus because he and all the saints that have gone on ahead is cheering you on. It might be dark, it might be lonely but know that you are not alone just keep your eyes on Jesus and see how he finished and know that you can finish also!

DAILY SCRIPTURES FOR MEDITATION

"Suppose one of you wants to build a tower. Won't you first sit down and estimate the cost to see if you have enough money to complete it? For if you lay, the foundation and are not able to finish it, everyone who sees it will ridicule you, saying, 'This person began to build and wasn't able to finish.' - Luke 14:28-30 (NIV)

Jesus said to them, My food (nourishment) is to do the will (pleasure) of Him Who sent Me and to accomplish and completely finish His work. - John 4:34 (AMPC)

But I have as My witness something greater (weightier, higher, better) than that of John; for the works that the Father has appointed Me to accomplish and finish, the very same works that I am now doing, are a witness and proof that the Father has sent Me. - John 5:36 (AMPC)

When Jesus had received the sour wine, He said, It is finished! And He bowed His head and gave up His spirit. - John 19:30 (AMPC)

Therefore then, since we are surrounded by so great a cloud of witnesses [who have borne testimony to the Truth], let us strip off and throw aside every encumbrance (unnecessary weight) and that sin which so readily (deftly and cleverly) clings to and entangles us, and let us run with patient endurance and steady and active persistence the appointed course of the race that is set before us,
Looking away [from all that will distract] to Jesus, Who is the Leader and the Source of our faith [giving the first incentive for our belief] and is also its Finisher [bringing it to maturity and perfection]. He, for the joy [of obtaining the prize] that was set before Him, endured the cross, despising and ignoring the shame, and is now seated at the right hand of the throne of God.
Just think of Him Who endured from sinners such grievous opposition and bitter hostility against Himself [reckon up and consider it all in comparison with your trials], so that you may not grow weary or exhausted, losing heart and relaxing and fainting in your minds. - Hebrews 12:1-3 (AMPC)

Day 3

The Apostle Paul Finished Strong

"Follow boldly in your Master's steps, for He has made this rough journey before you. Better a brief warfare and eternal rest than false peace and everlasting torment." - Alistair Begg

The Apostle Paul was a tremendous visionary, full of passion, and pursued his vision no matter the cost, but he didn't start off on the right track in his pursuit of souls. He was a Jew born to the tribe of Benjamin, and he was very educated in the Law of Moses. He was full of zeal for defending the law he held in high esteem. Therefore, he passionately pursued anyone that would seek to go against this law. He was notorious for persecuting the followers of Jesus because the gospel of Jesus Christ went against the spirit of religion.

One day Paul was on a mission to bring to prison all who would dare to follow Jesus Christ, but while on the way he had an encounter with God face to face that changed his course forever. In reality what happened was mind-boggling, and one could only reason it was God who brought about this sudden change. Paul went from one side of the spectrum to the opposite side; he would now become the persecuted rather than the persecutor - (Acts 9 NIV).

A new path was now charted for Paul, and he would have to count the cost of this call. He would have to decide if he would die for the cause of Christ, he knew of the opposition unleashed against the church of Christ, he was present at the stoning of an innocent follower of Jesus called Stephen. Paul was no stranger to the torment, pain, and persecution that awaited those who would dare associate with Jesus and his teachings. Never the less, Paul counted the cost and set out to start a new race, one that would change the course of the gentile world. Even though Paul was a Jew, he had a more significant impact on the Gentile nations, and he traveled extensively planting churches and feeding the body of Christ with wisdom from the Holy Spirit. Today two-thirds of the New Testament is written by the Apostle Paul because he counted the cost, he depended on the Holy Spirit for guidance and direction every step of the way. The Holy Spirit would reveal to him the persecutions he would face, the imprisonments, the beatings, the public humiliation, the loneliness, and even his death, but with all that he faced, he kept Jesus before him, and the will of the Father to make disciples of all men.

Paul could have chosen the life of the persecutor and gain status, position, and wealth but would have spent his eternity in torment. But after counting the cost, he chose not to gamble away eternity and headed to the starting line of the call that would cost him everything. I want to encourage you today to meditate on the life of Paul and weigh the choices before you; count the cost on both ends of the spectrum and see God move in and infuse you with strength as you chose his will!

DAILY SCRIPTURES FOR MEDITATION

"Suppose one of you wants to build a tower. Won't you first sit down and estimate the cost to see if you have enough money to complete it? For if you lay the foundation and are not able to finish it, everyone who sees it will ridicule you, saying, 'This person began to build and wasn't able to finish.' - Luke 14:28-30 (NIV)

Meanwhile, Saul was still breathing out murderous threats against the Lord's disciples. He went to the high priest and asked him for letters to the synagogues in Damascus, so that if he found any there who belonged to the Way, whether men or women, he might take them as prisoners to Jerusalem. As he neared Damascus on his journey, suddenly a light from heaven flashed around him. He fell to the ground and heard a voice say to him, "Saul, Saul, why do you persecute me?"
"Who are you, Lord?" Saul asked.
"I am Jesus, whom you are persecuting," he replied. "Now get up and go into the city, and you will be told what you must do."
The men traveling with Saul stood there speechless; they heard the sound but did not see anyone. Saul got up from the ground, but when he opened his eyes he could see nothing. So they led him by the hand into Damascus. For three days he was blind and did not eat or drink anything. - Acts 9-1:9 (NIV)
When the members of the Sanhedrin heard this, they were furious and gnashed their teeth at him. But Stephen, full of the Holy Spirit, looked up to heaven and saw the glory of God, and Jesus standing at

the right hand of God. "Look," he said, "I see heaven open and the Son of Man standing at the right hand of God."

At this they covered their ears and, yelling at the top of their voices, they all rushed at him, dragged him out of the city and began to stone him. Meanwhile, the witnesses laid their coats at the feet of a young man named Saul.

While they were stoning him, Stephen prayed, "Lord Jesus, receive my spirit." Then he fell on his knees and cried out, "Lord, do not hold this sin against them." When he had said this, he fell asleep. - Acts 7:54 - 60 (NIV)

"And now, compelled by the Spirit, I am going to Jerusalem, not knowing what will happen to me there. I only know that in every city the Holy Spirit warns me that prison and hardships are facing me. However, I consider my life worth nothing to me; my only aim is to finish the race and complete the task the Lord Jesus has given me— the task of testifying to the good news of God's grace. -Acts 20:22-24 (NIV)

Day 4

Finishing Declares Genuineness

"If I fail, I try again, and again, and again. If YOU fail, are you going to try again? The human spirit can handle much worse than we realize. It matters HOW you are going to FINISH. Are you going to finish strong?" - Nick Vujicic

The wisest king that lived, other than Jesus said, "The end of a matter is better than its beginning, and patience is better than pride."- (Ecclesiastes 7:8 NIV). When we ponder this thought, there is so much depth that lies within. Today, when we look around, it seems like every month there is a new line of clothing, bags, shoes, new miracle-working pills, slimming equipment, or countless cheap do it yourself gadgets, and the infomercials and commercials are endless, but after a few months we lose interest only to find something is new on the market. But when we look at the designer labels we know they get their title not only from their price, but because they have been around for years. They have worked hard and long to create a brand that can be trusted; their products are long-lasting and reliable. After many products have come and gone, these designers stand the test of time proving them to be genuine. So too it is with believers, when we stay the course, keep our eyes on Jesus and count the cost then our lives declare to the world that the Jesus we serve is real.

Anything that is counted as real and has excellent value must always pass a test. For example, let's take two students attending college, and they attended all the classes, but one of them decided not to take the final exam that would give him his certificate and the other did the exam and passed. Even though the person who didn't do the exam might know all the information to get a good job, without proof of passing the test, his education may not be real. When we look at the precious metal of gold, it goes through the melting process. According to UCSB ScienceLine, "The gold is heated in a furnace with silica, borax and soda ash which soaks up most of the impurities, forming a slag which rises to the top of the furnace while the heavier gold settles to the bottom." You see that even though the gold is gold unless it goes through the furnace of testing the genuineness and beauty, the gold will never be seen.

A test of time, trials, persecutions, delays, and obstacles are all considered time in the furnace, but as we see from the above testing, it is always necessary to show value and the genuineness. As we read through the pages of the Bible repeatedly, all the men went through great testing, trials, and persecution but through it all they have finished strong because they counted the cost, kept their eyes on their God, and until today the nation of Israel stands to prove to the world they are the nation separated unto God.

The Apostle Paul urged us to get rid of the heavy weight of sin or impurities that have only the ability to weigh us down – (Hebrews 12:1 - 2 NIV). He also encouraged us not to get tired in the journey but to keep doing good because the reward that awaits us is greater than the troubles we face in the present. Jesus received the reward of the souls he died for; The Apostle Paul received Jesus as his prize and added more souls to the kingdom of God. Today you will also receive Jesus, his strength, his grace, his mercy, his anointing, his wisdom, and his endurance to finish strong!

DAILY SCRIPTURES FOR MEDITATION

"Suppose one of you wants to build a tower. Won't you first sit down and estimate the cost to see if you have enough money to complete it? For if you lay the foundation and are not able to finish it, everyone who sees it will ridicule you, saying, 'This person began to build and wasn't able to finish.' - Luke 14:28-30 (NIV)

The end of a matter is better than its beginning, and patience is better than pride. - Ecclesiastes 7:8 (NIV)

Do you not know that in a race all the runners run, but only one gets the prize? Run in such a way as to get the prize. Everyone who competes in the games goes into strict training. They do it to get a crown that will not last, but we do it to get a crown that will last forever. Therefore I do not run like someone running aimlessly; I do not fight like a boxer beating the air. No, I strike a blow to my body and make it my slave so that after I have preached to others, I myself will not be disqualified for the prize. - 1 Corinthians 9:24-27 (NIV)

Therefore, since we are surrounded by such a great cloud of witnesses, let us throw off everything that hinders and the sin that so easily entangles. And let us run with perseverance the race marked out for us, fixing our eyes on Jesus, the pioneer and perfecter of faith. For the joy set before him, he endured the cross, scorning its shame, and sat down at the right hand of the throne of God. - Hebrews 12:1-2 (NIV)

being confident of this, that he who began a good work in you will carry it on to completion until the day of Christ Jesus. - Philippians 1:6 (NIV)

For I am already being poured out like a drink offering, and the time for my departure is near. I have fought the good fight, I have finished the race, I have kept the faith. Now there is in store for me the crown of righteousness, which the Lord, the righteous Judge, will award to me on that day—and not only to me but also to all who have longed for his appearing. - 2 Timothy 4:6-8 (NIV)

Reflections

Plan 7

GET YOUR PRAISE ON

===

What do you do in times of trials and tribulations? Do you become angry at God and ask why or do you praise your way through the storm? Praise is a powerful weapon that the children of God possess and it confuses the enemy of our soul. You have a choice- You can keep quiet in the trials, or you can use your voice to get your praise on and experience victory as the King of glory comes to your defense.

Day 1

You Have A Weapon

Every day in life we face challenges: be it in our homes, the job, in our relationships, health or finances. Every one of us is subject to battles, but the way we deal with our challenges will make the difference in the outcome. I find it very difficult to stay focused on God when my body is plagued with pain, or when my kids are failing a class, or even when my finances are running low. Perhaps you can identify with the struggle because we all know the struggle is real. Unfortunately, believers often get caught in the trap of the enemy by choosing the wrong point of focus which is the size of the problem. I have heard it said time and time again, "the battle is won or lost in the mind" and this to be very true because the apostle Paul admonishes us to renew our minds daily (Romans 12:2 NIV). Our thought life is so precious and important, and if we do not renew the mind, we are subject to give in to every desire and walk in fear and failure.

Our minds never seem blank at any time even when we are asleep; we still have sweet dreams and nightmares. According to an article by Carolyn Gregoire on "5 Amazing Things Your Brain Does While You Sleep" she stated,

"Research has identified a number of reasons sleep is critical to our health. When we're sleeping, the brain is anything but inactive. In fact, during sleep, neurons in the brain fire nearly as much as they do during waking hours — so it should come as no surprise that what happens during our resting hours is extremely important to a number brain and cognitive functions."

Imagine this; our mind is always at work, so we can reason we are becoming what we spend our time thinking on. I remember seeing a teaching by Joyce Meyer, "Where the mind goes, the man follows" now that is powerful, scary, and freeing simultaneously. I trust that as you are reading this plan revelation will come to you and you can take stock and identify what has been occupying your mind. Do you spend most of your time focusing on the problems in your life? Do you spend time often talking about your issues, pain, past hurts, and frustrations? Well from the information above, whatever you spend your time thinking about actually make its way even into your sleep time. God designed us to be consumed with him, but the enemy infiltrated, and now we spend our time thinking about us, our needs, our problems, our trials, our tribulations and a way out. While we may not have control of all the thoughts that run through our minds, we have the power to decide what stays, and our point of focus will determine where we end up. The good news is, God has not left us stranded but has empowered us with a weapon to combat every lie of the enemy, and it's called PRAISE!

"Satan so hates the genuine praise of Christ that his fiery darts of discouragement are not effective against us when we respond in praise." - William Thrasher

DAILY SCRIPTURES FOR MEDITATION

Do not conform to the pattern of this world, but be transformed by the renewing of your mind. Then you will be able to test and approve what God's will is—his good, pleasing and perfect will. - Romans 12:2 (NIV)

Finally, brothers and sisters, whatever is true, whatever is noble, whatever is right, whatever is pure, whatever is lovely, whatever is admirable—if anything is excellent or praiseworthy—think about such things. - Philippians 4:8 (NIV)

For the Lord takes delight in his people; he crowns the humble with victory.
Let his faithful people rejoice in this honor and sing for joy on their beds.
May the praise of God be in their mouths and a double-edged sword in their hands. - Psalm 149:4-6 (NIV)

Through Jesus, therefore, let us continually offer to God a sacrifice of praise—the fruit of lips that openly profess his name. - Hebrews 13:15 (NIV)

Therefore put on the full armor of God, so that when the day of evil comes, you may be able to stand your ground, and after you have done everything, to stand. - Ephesians 6:13 (NIV)

Day 2

Get The Promise

God's promises are true. He never disappoints on his promises. Disappointments come when we assume God should fulfill his promises to us on our timetable, and when it doesn't happen the way and time we want it to, that breeds hopelessness. One of the most heart-breaking situations in life is to have someone promise you something and then never follow through. But God will always bring to pass what he has promised. In the Bible there are promises for every obstacle and situation you may face in your life, the Apostle Paul tells us, "For no matter how many promises God has made, they are "Yes" in Christ. And so through him, the "Amen" is spoken by us to the glory of God." (2 Corinthians 1:20 NIV). A promise from God gives us hope to carry on even when the answer is delayed, or the enemy seems to make headway in destroying our lives.

One of my favorite stories in the Bible is about King Jehoshaphat, I know his name is long, but his story is astonishing and encouraging. King Jehoshaphat found himself nearly at war against an army much larger than his. How often the fight that comes to us is always more massive than we can handle, sometimes the mountains of problems seem so big, or the ocean of fears can be so deep, or the furnace can seem seven times hotter than usual. Perhaps your mountain is a divorce; your ocean is debt or your furnace is cancer or some other impossible situation but take heart because God has a promise for your situation. It is remarkable how people expect God to do something for them and yet, they do not understand if God promised it or not because they have not searched out his word. Remember, without a promise; there can be no real praise. We praise God because he is good and he does good.

When King Jehoshaphat got word of the impending battle, he purposed to hear from God, and he called all the people to gather together and fast and pray so they could seek an answer. When things seem hopeless it's time to call a few close friends and ask for prayer, maybe even fast a day and just seek God for an answer rather than worry yourself in fear and isolation. As the people gathered, the Spirit of the Lord spoke through Jahaziel, a priest, and God gave them a promise that day. God said,

"Listen, King Jehoshaphat and all who live in Judah and Jerusalem! This is what the Lord says to you: 'Do not be afraid or discouraged because of this vast army. For the battle is not yours, but God's. (2 Chronicles 20:15 NIV). The King got a promise from God, and now he could face the war at hand because he knew this was a battle only God could win. I pray you would seek a promise for your situation today.

"God never made a promise that was too good to be true" - D. L. Moody

DAILY SCRIPTURES FOR MEDITATION

For no matter how many promises God has made, they are "Yes" in Christ. And so through him, the "Amen" is spoken by us to the glory of God. - 2 Corinthians 1:20 (NIV)

The Lord is not slow in keeping his promise, as some understand slowness. Instead, he is patient with you, not wanting anyone to perish, but everyone to come to repentance. - 2 Peter 3:9 (NIV)

"As the heavens are higher than the earth, so are my ways higher than your ways. And my thoughts than your thoughts. As the rain and the snow come down from heaven, and do not return to it without watering the earth and making it bud and flourish, so that it yields seed for the sower and bread for the eater, so is my word that goes out from my mouth: It will not return to me empty, but will accomplish what I desire and achieve the purpose for which I sent it. You will go out in joy and be led forth in peace; the mountains and hills will burst into song before you and all the trees of the field will clap their hands. - Isaiah 55:9-11 (NIV)

Some people came and told Jehoshaphat, "A vast army is coming against you from Edom, from the other side of the Dead Sea. It is already in Hazezon Tamar" (that is, En Gedi). Alarmed, Jehoshaphat resolved to inquire of the Lord, and he proclaimed a fast for all Judah. The people of Judah came together to seek help from the Lord; indeed, they came from every town in Judah to seek him. - 2

Chronicles 20:2-4 (NIV)

Then the Spirit of the Lord came on Jahaziel, son of Zechariah, the son of Benaiah, the son of Jeiel, the son of Mattaniah, a Levite and descendant of Asaph, as he stood in the assembly.

He said: "Listen, King Jehoshaphat and all who live in Judah and Jerusalem! This is what the Lord says to you: 'Do not be afraid or discouraged because of this vast army. For the battle is not yours, but God's. Tomorrow march down against them. - 2 Chronicles 20:14 - 15 (NIV)

Day 3

Your Promise Fuels Your Praise

A promise from God is as good as it gets, there is no shortfall, no reneging, no changing his mind. God is just looking for someone who will take him at his word, and praise their way through because God will bring you out of your trouble, and he will lead you into all his goodness. The problem many of us face is the fight to believe God will come through. We read his word, we repeat and declare his promises, but we don't believe what we are saying. The Apostle James calls a person who prays but believes not double-minded man. I know when the situation seems enormous it is challenging to stay in faith, that is why God gives us a promise so we can recognize the answer forthcoming depends on him alone.

The Bible teaches us that God inhabits the praises of his people (Psalm 22:3 NIV). God is with us all the time in the person of the Holy Spirit, but when we praise God based on his goodness, faithfulness, and love for us, we experience a manifested presence of God where miracles can happen. So when we establish in our hearts God is who he says he is, the more faith we can express in his promises, and those promises will fuel our praise.

King Jehoshaphat got the promise from God, and he believed. He set out to do what God had told him. He gathered the people the next day and gave them a pep talk based on the promise he got from God, and they got ready to take their positions for war. It is marvelous the way God calls us to war, and it is not the way of the world. The Apostle Paul tells us our weapons are not carnal but mighty through God-(2 Corinthians 10:4 NIV). In every battle, we must learn to stand in faith believing God's promise, praise him, and he will show up and fight for you.

Armed with priests and singers, they were ready for battle. To the army on the other side this might have looked ridiculous on every level, they must have thought "We have the victory in this one" and probably laughed at the situation. But little did they know this army would not fight this battle in their own strength, but the God of the universe would show up and defend them. So too, know that God never changes, and if he did it back then for King Jehoshaphat, he would do it again for you. When all else is lost, when it looks impossible, as long as you have a promise from God, you are positioned for the victory as you stand and declare the goodness of your God. King Jehoshaphat did no war chant, but they stood and gave thanks to the Lord. They focused their praise on their God and how good, faithful, kind and loving he was, establishing that his qualities would last forever.

> *"When you need God to answer a prayer you ask God for a promise; and when God gives you a promise, having prayed for the promise, then you start to praise from the promise – pray for the promise and then praise from the promise."* - George Muller

DAILY SCRIPTURES FOR MEDITATION

But when you ask, you must believe and not doubt, because the one who doubts is like a wave of the sea, blown and tossed by the wind. That person should not expect to receive anything from the Lord. Such a person is double-minded and unstable in all they do. - James 1:6-8 (NIV)

Yet you are enthroned as the Holy One; You are the one Israel praises. - Psalm 22:3 (NIV)

The weapons we fight with are not the weapons of the world. On the contrary, they have divine power to demolish strongholds. - 2 Corinthians 10:4 (NIV)

Then some Levites from the Kohathites and Korahites stood up and praised the Lord, the God of Israel, with a very loud voice. Early in the morning, they left for the Desert of Tekoa. As they set out, Jehoshaphat stood and said, "Listen to me, Judah and people of Jerusalem! Have faith in the Lord your God, and you will be upheld; have faith in his prophets, and you will be successful." After consulting the people, Jehoshaphat appointed men to sing to the Lord and to praise him for the splendor of his holiness as they went out at the head of the army, saying:

"Give thanks to the Lord, for his love endures forever." -2 Chronicles

20:19-21 (NIV)

Day 4

The Enemy Is Allergic To Praise

Do you know the enemy cannot stand praise and worship? He hates a joyful believer, and if we persist in praising God instead of complaining about our problems, it drives the enemy mad, and he gets very confused. If only we could glimpse what happens in the kingdom of darkness, I think we would praise more and complain less. But if we look at the natural realm we can understand what praise does to the enemy. Have you ever hurt someone to the core? I mean that hurt should have taken a lifetime to get over, but during the time of anger and pain, the person seems to rise above it, they seem to dress better, they seem to get more attention than before and suddenly, you get upset, jealous, and even confused. Well multiply that feeling a million times over, and that is how the enemy gets when despite all you have been through you can still throw your hands up and give God praise.

Too often when we go to pray or praise, we focus our words on the enemy instead of our great God; diluting the warfare and that leaves us exhausted, frustrated, and defeated. If you have gotten hold of a promise from God, then it is time to stop shouting at the enemy. It is time to zone in on that promise and declare the greatness of your God. Go to your secret place of prayer and stand on that promise, and focus your praise on God and see him come into your situation and give you the victory. King David was also a man who faced many trials and tribulations in his life. He was anointed to be king in his teenage years, yet never took his throne until he was thirty, but in all his troubles he said, "I will bless the Lord at all time; His praise shall continually be in my mouth." (Psalm 34:1 NIV)

When King Jehoshaphat and his army went out to battle, they sang and praised. Their focus was on their God, and this caused God to show up. The story tells us, "As they began to sing and praise, the Lord set ambushes against the men of Ammon and Moab and Mount Seir who were invading Judah, and they were defeated." (2 Chronicles 20:22 NIV). How powerful is that?

Often we think we are fighting the enemy, but the truth is we are not; we invite God into our battle, and he fights for us. When I got hold of this revelation, it took a huge burden off my shoulders, and today I pray that your burden will also be lifted. Praise not only brought the people of Judah the victory, but it also brought them into great material blessings. My friends, everything we need is wrapped up in the person and presence of Jesus. I encourage you to turn your focus away from the enemy, and invite God into your situation, turn your gaze upon him, get your praise on, and watch him decimate the plans and purposes of the enemy.

> *"If the devil has ever troubled you, let me tell you this: you can trouble him a lot more than he troubles you when you learn to praise and glorify the Lord Jesus Christ in his presence. He hates it. It embarrasses him, he'll go somewhere else."* - Derek Prince

DAILY SCRIPTURES FOR MEDITATION

I will bless the Lord at all times; His praise shall continually be in my mouth. - Psalm 34:1 (AMPC)

After consulting the people, Jehoshaphat appointed men to sing to the Lord and to praise him for the splendor of his holiness as they went out at the head of the army, saying:
"Give thanks to the Lord, for his love endures forever."
As they began to sing and praise, the Lord set ambushes against the men of Ammon and Moab and Mount Seir who were invading Judah, and they were defeated. The Ammonites and Moabites rose up against the men from Mount Seir to destroy and annihilate them. After they finished slaughtering the men from Seir, they helped to destroy one another.
When the men of Judah came to the place that overlooks the desert and looked toward the vast army, they saw only dead bodies lying on the ground; no one had escaped. So Jehoshaphat and his men went to carry off their plunder, and they found among them a great amount of equipment and clothing and also articles of value—more than they could take away. There was so much plunder that it took three days to collect it. On the fourth day, they assembled in the Valley of Berakah, where they praised the Lord. This is why it is called the Valley of Berakah to this day. - 2 Chronicles 20:21-26 (NIV)

Sing to the Lord a new song, his praise from the ends of the earth, you who go down to the sea, and all that is in it, you islands, and all who live in them. Let the wilderness and its towns raise their voices; let the settlements where Kedar lives rejoice. Let the people of Sela sing for joy; let them shout from the mountaintops. Let them give glory to the Lord and proclaim his praise in the islands. The Lord will march out like a champion, like a warrior he will stir up his zeal; with a shout, he will raise the battle cry and will triumph over his enemies.
- Isaiah 42:10-13 (NIV)

Reflections

Plan 8

IDENTITY- WHO ARE YOU?

===

In the world, it's easy for us to question our identities and who we are. We try to fit in and be like everyone else, but the truth is -We are not! Who you are is wrapped up in one Person only, and his name is Jesus. As you read through this plan, I pray that you would find your true self- the one that God created you to be.

Day 1

Ask The Creator

As we look around the world, today people seem to search for the answer to whom they are and in the quest to understand their identity they go to the extreme to be different. Somehow being different becomes the priority. We identify identity with popularity, success, careers, relationships, education, position, status, geographical locations, economic backgrounds and the culture of the day just to list a few, and somehow we narrow down who we are by what we do or who we are associated with. The definition of identity is, "Who you are, the way you think about yourself, the way you are viewed by the world and the characteristics that define you. It also means the exact likeness in nature and qualities." I particularly like the last statement in the definition of identity because as a believer we do not find our identity in something, but instead, we find our identity in someone and his name is Jesus.

If we never realize that we are not what we do, we will forever chase every new fad and every new swing of the culture around us and that my friends will be a wilderness experience for the rest of our lives. We are so much more than the certificate we have hanging on our walls, we are so much more than the brand of clothes and shoes we wear, or the color of our skin, eyes or hair; yet the world seems to dictate to us who we should be by these very things.

For many years I struggled with my identity, born to an interracial couple, and then raised by a single parent, to living in an abusive home, to having no parents and having to become responsible for myself from a very young age. I struggled with my faith; wondering how a loving God could allow me to face all these different scenarios in one life. The struggle with my identity led me to make bad decisions because I was always looking to be made whole by things and people and I slipped further into the dictates and opinions of the world around me. But God had a plan all along, and I had to come to the end of my false sense of identity to face God like Moses did after he ran away from Egypt. In one day Moses went from being the prince of Egypt to a fugitive. Why? The answer is he was made for more but because he did not know who he was his actions defined him, until that day when he had the encounter with God in the burning bush. To understand who we are we must exhaust all our abilities, smarts, and self-sufficiency and face God to discover the truth about our identity.

You see only the manufacturer of a product can tell you conclusively about that product because they made it. So to discover who you are you must spend time with the one who made you. God knew you before you were formed in your mother's womb, he saw your whole life before you lived one day. So why not take a moment today to come to his feet, sit there a while and ask him about you. I am sure your heavenly father would love to have that face to face with you.

"God is the only one who has the authority to tell you who you are." Sarah Mae

DAILY SCRIPTURES FOR MEDITATION

Oh yes, you shaped me first inside, then out; you formed me in my mother's womb. I thank you; High God—you're breathtaking! Body and soul, I am marvelously made! I worship in adoration—what a creation! You know me inside and out, You know every bone in my body; you know exactly how I was made, bit by bit, How I was sculpted from nothing into something. Like an open book, you watched me grow from conception to birth; all the stages of my life were spread out before you, the days of my life all prepared before I'd even lived one day. - Psalm 139:13-16 (MSG)

"Before I shaped you in the womb, I knew all about you. Before you saw the light of day, I had holy plans for you: A prophet to the nations that's what I had in mind for you." - Jeremiah 1:5 (MSG)

Day 2

Who Are You?

I trust that after spending time with the Creator yesterday, you are intrigued to go deeper into the answer to your identity. Every day as you read this plan I want you to remember this statement, "exact likeness in nature and qualities," from the definition of identity we looked at yesterday. We established that our identity is not wrapped up in what we do but is in the person of Jesus Christ; therefore to know who we are, we must now understand who he is. In the book of Genesis and the story of creation, we see how God the Father created everything by the spoken word, but with the first man, God got involved. He did not speak man into existence, but used his hands and dust from the ground to mold and gave shape to the form of man.

After God formed man it was only a shape, but it was not alive, and God did not speak the man into life. I get so excited about the awesomeness of humans, imagine with me for a moment God took a deep breath in and then God blew into the nostrils of man and suddenly, the dead form became alive. The Bible says, "The man came alive – a living soul" (Genesis 2:7 MSG). God released a part of himself into man and man became alive.

You are not what you do, but the answer to who you are is – "You are a living soul". I was not spoken into existence, but I was formed and shaped by the very hand of God, and then the very breath of God makes me alive and continues to sustain me. I get overwhelmed every time I ponder the thought of who I am. It should then come as no surprise what the enemy of our soul better known as Satan is after - our identity!

Being a living soul sets us apart from the rest of creation and from this point of understanding, we are then enabled to function in our God-given purpose. I often used the excuse of, "I'm only human" to cover my mistakes and live outside my purpose, and the enemy loves it when we downplay what being human means. Being a living soul allows me to commune and have fellowship with God, it enables me to make intelligent and godly decisions and choices, it allows me to have emotions and be moved with compassion and most of all it entitles me to be like Jesus. We are made in the image and likeness of

God, all humans are made with a soul, and the soul consists of the mind, will, and emotions. We can think, we have senses to access this natural realm, and we can choose. As you sit at Heavenly Father's feet today may you ponder on the truth that God's very breath is sustaining you right now and celebrate that you are a living soul!

"If we take our meaning in life from our family, our work, a cause, or some achievement other than God they enslave us"
Tim Keller

DAILY SCRIPTURES FOR MEDITATION

God spoke: "Let us make human beings in our image, make them reflecting our nature So they can be responsible for the fish in the sea, the birds in the air, the cattle, And, yes, Earth itself, and every animal that moves on the face of the Earth."
God created human beings; he created them godlike, Reflecting God's nature. He created them male and female. God blessed them:
"Prosper! Reproduce! Fill Earth! Take charge! Be responsible for fish in the sea and birds in the air,
For every living thing that moves on the face of the Earth." - Genesis 1:26-28 (MSG)

At the time God made Earth and Heaven, before any grasses or shrubs had sprouted from the ground—God hadn't yet sent rain on Earth, nor was there anyone around to work the ground (the whole Earth was watered by underground springs)—God formed Man out of dirt from the ground and blew into his nostrils the breath of life. The Man came alive—a living soul! - Genesis 2:5 - 7 (MSG)

Day 3

The Enemy Of Your Soul

Now that you have taken the time to grasp you are so much more than what you do or what you possess let us look at the one after our identity. When we look at the creation of man we recognize that first God made man in his image giving man a part of his own life and God called the man a living soul. God identified the man as having his image and likeness then he told man what his duties were - (Genesis 1:28 MSG). So we can reason that God identified man as like him and then set him on his duties. Adam and Eve were not identified by their job description they were identified as in God's image and likeness. We should understand our identity is in God because the enemy of our souls understands our identity better than we know.

Before man was created, it is believed by many scholars that Lucifer was an archangel of God and he was described as being beautiful and in charge of worship in heaven. He held a major position in heaven putting him near God. But the Bible tells us pride was in him, and he wanted the place of God which led to his removal both from his high position and beauty to the dark realm. So when God created man in his image and likeness, it angered Satan, and his primary focus now was to destroy the sons of God. He is relentless in making sure as sons of God we never understand who we are and the power provided to us through this covenant blood of Jesus Christ. In perfection, Satan found a way in to entice and enslave Adam and Eve with his lies. He is described as a thief, a murderer and a destroyer (John 10:10 NIV). He is also called our enemy, a fake lion (1 Peter 5:8 NIV). He is called a hater of truth (John 8:44 NIV).

With such strong titles, he is not kidding about hating us or going easy on us; he is very subtle and cunning. He does not make himself known as evil but presents himself through thoughts that are weaved with lies and some truth; he loves to make us reason, doubt and question God's character and word. As long as he is speaking, he is lying because he is the father of lies. (John 8:44 NIV). He will stop at nothing to make sure you never come into your identity in Christ, but I am thankful that God will open your eyes to see yourself with value and worth in Christ Jesus. As you sit at your Heavenly Father's feet today, ponder the magnitude of your identity and ask Abba to help you recognize the enemy of your soul so you can stand firm whenever he lurks to pull you away from who you are.

"The enemy of our soul thrives on keeping us in darkness and unable to live in the fullness God created us to be." - Dr. Michelle Bengtson.

DAILY SCRIPTURES FOR MEDITATION

The word of the Lord came to me: "Son of man, take up a lament concerning the king of Tyre and say to him: 'this is what the Sovereign Lord says:'"You were the seal of perfection, full of wisdom and perfect in beauty. You were in Eden, the garden of God; every precious stone adorned you: carnelian, chrysolite, and emerald, topaz, onyx, and jasper, lapis lazuli, turquoise, and beryl. Your settings and mountings were made of gold; on the day you were created they were prepared. You were anointed as a guardian cherub, for so I ordained you. You were on the holy mount of God; you walked among the fiery stones. You were blameless in your ways from the day you were created till wickedness was found in you. Through your widespread trade you were filled with violence, and you sinned. So I drove you in disgrace from the mount of God, and I expelled you, guardian cherub, from among the fiery stones. Your heart became proud on account of your beauty, and you corrupted your wisdom because of your splendor. So I threw you to the earth; I made a spectacle of you before kings. - Ezekiel 28:11-17 (NIV)

How you have fallen from heaven, morning star, son of the dawn! You have been cast down to the earth, you who once laid low the nations! You said in your heart, "I will ascend to the heavens; I will raise my throne above the stars of God; I will sit enthroned on the mount of assembly, on the utmost heights of Mount Zaphon. I will ascend above the tops of the clouds; I will make myself like the Most High." But you are brought down to the realm of the dead, to the depths of the pit. - Isaiah 14:12-15 (NIV)

The thief comes only to steal and kill and destroy; I have come that they may have life, and have it to the full. - John 10:10 (NIV)

Be well balanced (temperate, sober of mind), be vigilant and cautious at all times; for that enemy of yours, the devil, roams around like a lion roaring [in fierce hunger], seeking someone to seize upon and devour. - 1 Peter 5:8 (AMPC)

You belong to your father, the devil, and you want to carry out your father's desires. He was a murderer from the beginning, not holding to the truth, for there is no truth in him. When he lies, he speaks his native language, for he is a liar and the father of lies. - John 8:44 (NIV)

Day 4

The Scandal Of Identity Theft

Lies, disobedience, disgrace, disappointment, hurt, shame, separation, tears, curses, death, and darkness all make up a scandal. This scandal happened in the place of perfection, beauty, bliss, provision, peace, and rest. One would think in such paradise the enemy of our souls could never reach us there. Wrong! He found a way into perfection because we are made in God's image and likeness we are separated from all other creation because we can choose and that is the power of a human. The one thing the enemy of our soul is good at is lying, and he infiltrated his way into paradise to destroy it. Mind you, the enemy never grandly entrances with the red cape, red underwear, two horns and a pitchfork to tempt us but instead presents himself in a form of being accepted, he whispers thoughts into our minds to cause doubt of God's word to enter.

In the Garden of Eden, God gave freely of every tree for food, but one particular tree he told them not to eat from because there were consequences attached to it - namely death - (Genesis 2:15 – 17 NIV). God told them specifically the result of eating from the tree. Death would be enough for me not to eat from that tree yet today we know many consequences to sin, however, we still indulge if we give in to the thoughts and lies of the enemy. Let us take it step by step:

1 – God made his children in his image and likeness breathing his very breath into them.

2 – God identified them as made in his image and likeness.

3 – God then told them who they were, and then he instructed them how they were to function for daily life and also asked them to stay away from one tree that could threaten their lives.

4 – The enemy of their souls found a way into paradise and starts a conversation about identity with the woman close to that tree.

The Bible tells us the enemy goes about like a roaring lion looking for an opportunity to pounce. I am sure Adam and Eve spent time at the other trees in the garden, but somehow the enemy showed up at the right time just when they were there. He was studying their every move and waited for the opportune time to make his sales pitch. Then he presented his lies that caused Eve to doubt God's word and stole her identity. He offered her the privilege of becoming like God if she would eat of the forbidden tree. He was offering her an identity she already had, she was already made in God's image and likeness yet he told her she would be like God and she would not die if she ate. As Eve believed his lies and partook of the fruit and indulged her husband; at that moment they gave up life and introduced death because of disobedience. The natural balance of everything created was affected, and now separation from God was in effect. As you sit at your heavenly Father feet today, thank him for showing you the power to choose is available and ask him to help you make the right choices knowing you are his child.

"God has a plan for your life. The enemy has a plan for your life. Be ready for both just be wise enough to know which one to battle and which one to embrace." BibleGodQuotes.com

DAILY SCRIPTURES FOR MEDITATION

The Lord God took the man and put him in the Garden of Eden to work it and take care of it. And the Lord God commanded the man, "You are free to eat from any tree in the garden; but you must not eat from the tree of the knowledge of good and evil, for when you eat from it, you will certainly die." - Genesis 2:15-17 (NIV)

Now the serpent was more crafty than any of the wild animals the Lord God had made. He said to the woman, "Did God really say, 'You must not eat from any tree in the garden'?"
The woman said to the serpent, "We may eat fruit from the trees in the garden, but God did say, 'you must not eat fruit from the tree that is in the middle of the garden, and you must not touch it, or you will die.'"
"You will not certainly die," the serpent said to the woman.
"For God knows that when you eat from it, your eyes will be opened, and you will be like God, knowing good and evil."
When the woman saw that the fruit of the tree was good for food and pleasing to the eye, and also desirable for gaining wisdom, she took

some and ate it. She also gave some to her husband, who was with her, and he ate it. - Genesis 3:1-6 (NIV)

Leave no [such] room or foothold for the devil [give no opportunity to him]. - Ephesians 4:27 (AMPC)

Day 5

System Corrupted

The lies were presented to Eve, she gave in and ate the forbidden fruit and immediately put the death of everything in motion. I like to think of it as a computer program running and functioning well, but somehow a virus finds its way to the computer and presents itself as a solution to fix a non-existent problem. Without careful consideration of the authenticity of the presenter, one accepts the solution and downloads a virus and corrupts the whole system. It causes the computer to slow down; it destroys crucial information that sometimes can never be retrieved and the purpose is to steal and destroy the hard-drive eventually. Well, this took place with Adam and Eve their thoughts become corrupted, their souls became conflicted and spiritual death, and separation from God entered ultimately leading to physical death.

They gave up their identity, and now they saw themselves naked, ashamed, they were introduced to fear, but even in this state, we see the grace of God still being provided to them. God loved them, and I know it must have wrenched his heart to see the separation that would now come between him and his beloved children. In his marvelous grace and mercy God did what he had to do to protect them, and now a life had to be taken to clothe and cover them. They had to leave the garden because the tree of life would now pose another threat to them, had they eaten of the tree of life in their sin condition they would have remained separated from God forever, and God's love could not bear to separate from them forever.

When God addressed them on why they disobeyed, the blame game started, and Adam blamed God for the woman he was given, Eve blamed the serpent, and no one would take responsibility for their actions. Only when we come to the place of taking responsibility for our actions would we be on a path to restoring our identity. I lived many years playing the part of the victim because my dad left when I was a baby, I was abused and rejected, and I blamed the world, leaders, teachers and anyone I thought I could pass the blame to. Because of the blame game, I lost many years of my life trying to be someone else, and I hated myself, the self I thought was worthless.

But there was a day in my life I found the savior, and he led me to accept the past, let the mistakes go and embrace who I am in him. Today as you sit at your Father's feet, ask him for the strength to let go of the victim mentality, the blame game and to take responsibility for the bad decisions and poor choices. Release it today because the God who created you is waiting to restore you to your true identity.

> *"The major strategy of Satan is to distort the character of God and the truth of who we are. He can't change God, and he can't do anything to change our identity and position in Christ. If, however, he can get us to believe a lie, we will live as though our identity in Christ isn't true."* - Neil T. Anderson

DAILY SCRIPTURES FOR MEDITATION

Then the eyes of both of them were opened, and they realized they were naked; so they sewed fig leaves together and made coverings for themselves.
Then the man and his wife heard the sound of the Lord God as he was walking in the garden in the cool of the day, and they hid from the Lord God among the trees of the garden. But the Lord God called to the man, "Where are you?"
He answered, "I heard you in the garden, and I was afraid because I was naked; so I hid."
And he said, "Who told you that you were naked? Have you eaten from the tree that I commanded you not to eat from?"
The man said, "The woman you put here with me—she gave me some fruit from the tree, and I ate it."
Then the Lord God said to the woman, "What is this you have done?
"The woman said, "The serpent deceived me, and I ate." - Genesis 3:7 -13 (NIV)

Day 6

Claim Back Your Identity

Adam the first man made a choice that hurt the human race but with God's grace, kindness and mercy a way was made for the second Adam (Jesus) to come to earth and face a choice to become sin for us and defeat death or turn his back on us and chose his will. I am very grateful for the choice Jesus made to become sin for me so I can live with him forever. Jesus' death and resurrection opened the door for fellowship and communication with the Heavenly Father again. Now, the enemy of our soul can still try to lie to us as he did to Eve but we have the same choice as she did and we can choose differently. We can claim our identity in Christ and his finished work on the cross which he paid in full for our identity to be restored. Unfortunately, we deal with an enemy that will not give us a break till he is finally bound in hell, so he still looks for idle minds to spin his web of lies on.

The good news is the Apostle Paul tells us how we can maintain our identity in Christ.

He said, Do not be conformed to this world (this age), [fashioned after and adapted to its external, superficial customs], but be transformed (changed) by the [entire] renewal of your mind [by its new ideals and its new attitude], so you may prove [for yourselves] what is the good and acceptable and perfect will of God, even the thing which is good and acceptable and perfect [in His sight for you]. Romans 12:2 (AMPC)

According to Strong's Concordance, the word "conformed" in the Greek is "suschematizo," and it means "identified with," "having outward shape" or "assuming a similar outward form (expression) by following the same pattern (model, mold)."

The Apostle Paul was telling us, do not just fit into the mold or model of our culture, don't just take on an outward shape to be like everyone else; living life based on the ever-changing culture of the day or peoples shifting opinions. But be transformed, be changed, and it all takes place in the mind.

The word transformed in the Greek is "metamorphoo," and it means "change after being with," changing form in keeping with inner reality" or "transfigured." This word is also where we get the English word "metamorphosis" – that process that takes place in a butterfly's life, a complete transformation from one form to another all the while staying true to our identity.

I am always in awe about the magnitude of our true identity as believers. The enemy longs to lie to us and tell us we will forever be ugly, shameful and worthless; we need not accept that lie because the truth is we are still made in the image and likeness of God. We become what we worship, and we become like the people we spend time with! The Apostle Paul emphasizes to stay true to our God-identity we must spend time in the word of God constantly filling our minds with his truth and we will become like the ONE we spend time with – Our Savior. As you sit at your Heavenly Father's feet today, ask him to remove all veils and blindness to his words and may you embrace truth and be transformed into the beautiful butterfly that's deep within.

"The Gospel is not an invitation to imitate Jesus Christ. The Gospel is an invitation to be transformed by Jesus Christ." - Alistair Begg

DAILY SCRIPTURES FOR MEDITATION

God made him who had no sin to be sin for us so that in him we might become the righteousness of God. - 2 Corinthians 5:21 (NIV)

So it is written: "The first man Adam became a living being"; the last Adam, a life-giving spirit. - 1 Corinthians 15:45 (NIV)

Do not be conformed to this world (this age), [fashioned after and adapted to its external, superficial customs], but be transformed (changed) by the [entire] renewal of your mind [by its new ideals and its new attitude], so that you may prove [for yourselves] what is the good and acceptable and perfect will of God, even the thing which is good and acceptable and perfect [in His sight for you]. - Romans 12:2 (AMPC)

And we all, who with unveiled faces contemplate the Lord's glory, are being transformed into his image with ever-increasing glory, which comes from the Lord, who is the Spirit. - 2 Corinthians 3:18 (NIV)

Reflections

Plan 9

LAUNCH OUT INTO THE DEEP

==

When I think about the deep, the ocean immediately comes to mind- vast and beautiful yet with so many unknowns it challenges my ability to be in control, and that is a feeling that many of us don't like. However, you were never created to play in the shallow. God has a massive plan for your life, and he wants to speak to you today to expand your view, to take the limits off, shatter the fear that has kept you back and trust him in this next phase of your life.

Day 1

What Is Your Ocean?

I love to stand on the seashore and look out as far as my eyes can take me on the vast ocean as it stretches to meet the sky, and the thoughts of what is contained deep within the ocean ravish my mind. The ocean is beautiful but I have always had a fear of the deep, being surrounded by so much water, with so many unknowns that challenge my ability to be in control, and that is a feeling I don't like. I know from reading books, stories I've been told, movies and documentaries I've watched, they all tell me there is so much more to see and experience in the deep, but my fear of losing control, my fear of not seeing or navigating my way, the fear of being open to attacks keeps me from venturing out for more. Have you ever felt this way? The ocean is just an example of the width and depth of the life God has for us as believers; the ocean gives us a visual of the inexhaustible life of grace, love, mercy, kindness, blessings, and opportunities that awaits us when we enter new life with Christ.

What is your ocean today? What do you see when you stand on the shores of your life and look out till your ocean meets the horizon? What opportunities await you in the deep? What fears plague your minds as you stand contemplating should I turn and walk away or should I launch out and trust God? The ocean is one of Earth's most valuable natural resources; it provides food in fish, it's used for transportation, it provides a treasured source of recreation for humans and great beauty, and great wealth exists in the deep. If we are not venturing out into the deep, it means we are in the shallow, and there is not much to explore in the shallow. There is no depth, and our view of life becomes superficial when we remain where we are in control. Nothing of significance can grow, survive, or be sustained in the shallow because the waves of life will always wash away and diminish that which had no roots.

You were not created to spend your whole life on the sandy shores watching others venture out into the deep while you only dream of what "could be." God has placed an ocean size dream in our hearts for our lives, and it's a life that hinges on faith in him. While we may not know or have all the facts, directions, pit stops, obstacles, storms, and attacks we rest in the ONE who made the ocean and has written the script for our lives. Perhaps you have never viewed your life as an ocean before, but I believe you did not choose this plan by chance. God wants to speak to you today to expand your view, to take the limits off, shatter the fear that has kept you back and trust him in this next phase of your life.

"We gain strength and courage, and confidence by each experience in which we really stop to look fear in the face...we must do that which we think we cannot." –Eleanor Roosevelt

DAILY SCRIPTURES FOR MEDITATION

Who is like you, Lord God Almighty? You, Lord, are mighty, and your faithfulness surrounds you.
You rule over the surging sea; When its waves mount up, you still them. - Psalm 89:8-9 (NIV)

Should you not fear me?" declares the Lord. "Should you not tremble in my presence? I made the sand a boundary for the sea,
An everlasting barrier it cannot cross. The waves may roll, but they cannot prevail; they may roar, but they cannot cross it. - Jeremiah 5:22 (NIV)

The purposes of a person's heart are deep waters, but one who has insight draws them out. - Proverbs 20:5 (NIV)

Day 2

Get The Promise

As we read yesterday, launching out into the deep is a terrifying step, and if we have no promise from God, well that will just be disastrous. Living the abundant life that Jesus died to give us is sustained through his words, his promises, and his covenant with us. Spending time daily in fellowship and communion with the Lord is vital to receiving his counsel and guidance for the journey. Without the "*secret place*" moments with God, we can never face our fears and launch out into the deep. I spent many years of my life in the shallow because I would run after every idea that sounded good in my mind. I prayed for God's blessings on what I was doing but I never waited for him, I never spent time seeking his promises and as you can guess I was plagued with failure on every side. I basically would ask God to bless my plans, but I never heard his command or grasped his promises.

The Apostle Peter heard God's command one day while he was on the shores of the ocean. Peter and his friends had left their boats on the shore and went to wash their nets because they had a failed night of fishing. Peter made his living by fishing, this was his bread and butter, but he had a discouraging night at work. Jesus was teaching, and the people were pressing him, so he used Peter's boat as his pulpit, and he asked Peter to push him out a little so he can sit and teach the people on the shores. In Peter's willingness to allow Jesus to use his boat and to sit and listen to the teaching Peter found the faith to take hold of the command of Jesus. The Bible tells us, '"When he had finished speaking, he said to Simon, "Put out into deep water, and let down the nets for a catch."' (Luke 5:4 NIV). When we wait on God and listen to his words, we will hear his command and see his promises come to pass.

God has a good plan for your life, but before you venture out into the deep, I want to encourage you to spend time on the shores and just listen to him. I had felt the call to Pastor since I was sixteen years old but that call came to reality twenty-two years later, within that time I did everything to run from that call. One day, after running away and failing I went to Israel on the Holy land tour, and it was there on the Sea of Galilee while on a boat ride I heard God say, "Now is the time to launch out into the deep." It has been the best decision I have ever made, and it came when I stopped long enough to hear his command. Are you willing to wait on the shores and listen to God's command today?

"Your potential is the sum of all the possibilities God has for your life." –Charles Stanley

DAILY SCRIPTURES FOR MEDITATION

For I know the plans I have for you," declares the Lord, "plans to prosper you and not to harm you, plans to give you hope and a future. - Jeremiah 29:11 (NIV)

"As the heavens are higher than the earth, so are my ways higher than your ways and my thoughts than your thoughts. As the rain and the snow come down from heaven, and do not return to it without watering the earth and making it bud and flourish, so it yields seed for the sower and bread for the eater, so is my word that goes out from my mouth: It will not return to me empty, but will accomplish what I desire and achieve the purpose for which I sent it. - Isaiah 55:9-11 (NIV)

Day 3

Little Faith – Big Catch

Once we get hold of the command of God, there will be no stopping the plans God has for us. Will it be easy? Oh heavens no, but that is the reason for the promise; in difficult times we can trust the One who made the promise to keep his word. After Peter had fished all night and caught nothing I am sure he was tired and frustrated, he was a professional fisherman, and Jesus was a carpenter. I think in Peter's mind he was more of an expert of the navigation of the Sea of Galilee than Jesus because he had probably worked those waters all his life. Don't we all feel like that sometimes? When we have given all our years to a career, a relationship, business, or a ministry and all we come up with in the end is disappointments and loss; we just don't want to try anymore. God's words sometimes fall into hearts that are so broken and disillusioned that we have to muster up every ounce of faith to try again. Peter experienced this same feeling, the same discouragement, and loss but after hearing Jesus teach, he mustered up whatever little faith he had and, Simon answered, "Master, we've worked hard all night and haven't caught anything. But because you say so, I will let down the nets." (Luke 5:5 NIV)

Peter acted on the word in obedience even though all his natural senses were saying otherwise and in this act of obedience and submission to God's word, Peter experienced a huge miracle. The story says the catch in the deep was so enormous their nets broke, and they had to call other fishermen to help with the haul, but the nets not only broke, but their boat sank – "When they had done so, they caught such a large number of fish that their nets began to break. So they signaled their partners in the other boat to come and help them, and they came and filled both boats so full that they began to sink." (Luke 5: 6 – 7 NIV). What a miracle Peter experienced because of faith in the Promise Keeper! What if Peter just walked away and stood his ground he knew the waters and Jesus weren't qualified to give advice? Sometimes we don't want to take that step forward because of the failure, hurts, and disappointments are just too much, but I trust you will draw strength from Peter's story and muster up the little mustard seed faith and launch out into the deep. I pray that your haul will be tremendous and the miracle of your life will exude Jesus to the world around you.

"If God is your partner, make your plans BIG!" –D.L. Moody

DAILY SCRIPTURES FOR MEDITATION

One day as Jesus was standing by the Lake of Gennesaret, the people were crowding around him and listening to the word of God. He saw at the water's edge two boats, left there by the fishermen, who were washing their nets. He got into one boat, the one belonging to Simon, and asked him to put out a little from shore. Then he sat down and taught the people from the boat.
When he had spoken to the crowd, he said to Simon, "Put out into deep water, and let down the nets for a catch."
Simon answered, "Master, we've worked hard all night and haven't caught anything. But because you say so, I will let down the nets." - Luke 5:1 - 5 (NIV)

When they had done so, they caught many fish that their nets broke. So they signaled their partners in the other boat to come and help them, and they came and filled both boats so full they sank.
When Simon Peter saw this, he fell at Jesus' knees and said, "Go away from me, Lord; I am a sinful man!" For he and all his companions were astonished at the catch of fish they had taken, and so were James and John, the sons of Zebedee, Simon's partners.
Then Jesus said to Simon, "Don't be afraid; from now on you will fish for people." So they pulled their boats up on shore, left everything and followed him. - Luke 5:6 - 11 (NIV)

Day 4

Keep Your Eyes On The Horizon

The story of simple obedience to God's command prove so powerful in the Apostle Peter's life, but there is also another story in the Bible I love that shows the same principle of launching out into the deep. It's the story of Abraham, and I am sure you are no stranger to this great man of faith; after all, we are children of father Abraham. I hope his story will also inspire you to keep your eyes on the promise God has made to you. Abraham was called by God to leave his family and the place he was familiar with and venture on a journey to a land God would show him.

God only gave Abraham a command and a promise, and Abraham simply obeyed. The promise he received sounded so good, there was no reason for Abraham not to launch out. The Lord said, "I will make you into a great nation, and I will bless you, I will make your name great, and you will be a blessing. I will bless those who bless you, and whoever curses you I will curse, and all peoples on earth will be blessed through you." (Genesis 12:2 – 3 NIV). Who doesn't want to be rich and famous? It sounds like a great deal one I would not have passed up.

Unlike Peter who experienced his miracle immediately after he followed Jesus' command, Abraham's journey would be a long one. Sometimes, we receive what we ask for in a flash, and then sometimes, we must "Faith it till we make it." I think we would all prefer the Peter experience, but God has much to teach us in the Abraham experience. God gave Abraham the promise, but he never told Abraham the land he would give him was already occupied, he didn't tell him he would run into a famine and have to move, he didn't tell him he would experience separation from his nephew, or he would have to go to war. God also promised Abraham a son in his old age, but he didn't tell him he would have to wait about twenty-five years for that fulfillment and even after he had his son, God asked him to sacrifice his son after he waited that long. Just writing this makes me appreciate father Abraham, he wasn't perfect, he had his down and doubtful days, but through all that he faced, he kept his eyes on the horizon – the promises God made to him. He was drafted into the great hall of faith in the book of Hebrews because of his ability to take God at His word even when he could not see it happening.

Perhaps you have received a powerful word from God about your life, but so many obstacles and hindrances have happened along the way, and you think it won't happen for you. I want to encourage you to hold on to the stories of the men of faith in the Bible and keep your eyes on the horizon, and like Abraham, you too will see a beautiful end.

"God never said that the journey would be easy, but He did say that the arrival would be worthwhile" – Max Lucado.

DAILY SCRIPTURES FOR MEDITATION

Now there was a famine in the land, and Abram went down to Egypt to live there for a while because the famine was severe. - Genesis 12:10 (NIV)

Now Lot, who was moving about with Abram, also had flocks and herds and tents. But the land could not support them while they stayed together, for their possessions were so great they could not stay together. And quarreling arose between Abram's herders and Lot's. The Canaanites and Perizzites were also living in the land.
So Abram said to Lot, "Let's not have any quarreling between you and me, or between your herders and mine, for we are close relatives. Is not the whole land before you? Let's part company. If you go to the left, I'll go to the right; if you go to the right, I'll go to the left." - Genesis 13:5-9 (NIV)

When Abram heard that his relative had been taken captive, he called out the 318 trained men born in his household and went in pursuit as far as Dan. During the night Abram divided his men to attack them, and he routed them, pursuing them as far as Hobah, north of Damascus. He recovered all the goods and brought back his relative Lot and his possessions, with the women and the other people. - Genesis 14:14-16 (NIV)

After this, the word of the Lord came to Abram in a vision: "Do not be afraid, Abram.

I am your shield, your very great reward."

But Abram said, "Sovereign Lord, what can you give me since I remain childless and the one who will inherit my estate is Eliezer of Damascus?" And Abram said, "You have given me no children; so a servant in my household will be my heir."

Then the word of the Lord came to him: "This man will not be your heir, but a son who is your own flesh and blood will be your heir." He took him outside and said, "Look up at the sky and count the stars— if indeed you can count them." Then he said to him, "So shall your offspring be."

Abram believed the Lord, and he credited it to him as righteousness.
- Genesis 15: 1 - 6 (NIV)

Sometime later God tested Abraham. He said to him, "Abraham!"

"Here I am," he replied.

Then God said, "Take your son, your only son, whom you love— Isaac—and go to the region of Moriah. Sacrifice him there as a burnt offering on a mountain I will show you." - Genesis 22: 1 - 2 (NIV)

By faith Abraham, when called to go to a place he later receive as his inheritance, obeyed and went, even though he did not know where he was going. By faith he made his home in the promised land like a stranger in a foreign country; he lived in tents, as did Isaac and Jacob, who were heirs with him of the same promise. For he was looking forward to the city with foundations, whose architect and builder is God. And by faith, even Sarah, who was past childbearing age, was enabled to bear children because she considered him faithful who had made the promise. And so from this one man, and he as good as dead, came descendants as numerous as the stars in the sky and as countless as the sand on the seashore. - Hebrews 11: 8 - 12 (NIV)

Reflections

Plan 10

LOVE IS GOD'S LANGUAGE

==

In the world, Love has become so misunderstood and misused by not only the people of the world but also by believers. Love has lost its value and significance to many, but as you read through this plan, I pray that you will have a revelation of what Love is and its true meaning.

Day 1

God Is Love

For most of my life I grew up hearing how angry God was with his creation especially humans and while I longed to serve and please God, I did it from a very unhealthy place of fear. I heard a lot about what was upsetting God and how my actions were causing his anger. I grew up without a father in my early years and then, later on, I lived with my stepfather who only caused further despair and damage to my view of a father figure. Besides my personal experiences and the teachings of God being angry all the time created a very warped view of love and more so the love of a male figure in my life.

My approach to God was one of a distant relationship and as I mentioned my experiences with my earthly father figures made me comfortable with the view it was better to serve God from a distance and be content that if I didn't get everything right, I could expect judgment in my life. I lived with an expectation that things will always go wrong in my life because of the underlying truth I could not keep all God's commands, and just like my earthly father's dealing with me I could expect God the Father to do the same. I lived a very chaotic, depressed and hopeless life all the while being in the church.

I know the above scenario may not be so strange to many of you reading this plan and I hope that if you are still thinking or feeling this way about God the Father that your mindset will be changed and you will be set free from the bondage of fear. The scriptures declare, "God is love" (1 John 4:8 NIV). In 1 John 4:7 – 21 the words love, loves and loved is mentioned approximately twenty-seven times and the author; the Apostle John called himself the "Disciple whom God loved." (John 13:23 NIV). The Apostle John had such a profound revelation about the love of God he endured many hardships and persecutions. Without a revelation of who God is and how much he loves us it will be easy for the storms, trials, and persecutions of life to beat us down and keep us in fear of judgment and condemnation. The enemy of our soul thrives on keeping us ignorant of God's love to derail us from being all God made us to be. I trust today will be a new beginning for you as you venture out to see God as loving and kind and be led to fulfill your purpose in this life.

Declaration: God is love, God is Love, God is Love!

DAILY SCRIPTURES FOR MEDITATION

Dear friends, let us love one another, for love comes from God. Everyone who loves has been born of God and knows God. Whoever does not love does not know God, because God is love. This is how God showed his love among us: He sent his one and only Son into the world that we might live through him. This is love: not that we loved God, but that he loved us and sent his Son as an atoning sacrifice for our sins. Dear friends, since God so loved us, we also ought to love one another. No one has ever seen God; but if we love one another, God lives in us and his love is made complete in us. - 1 John 4:7-12 (NIV)

This is how we know that we live in him and he in us: He has given us of his Spirit. And we have seen and testify that the Father has sent his Son to be the Savior of the world. If anyone acknowledges that Jesus is the Son of God, God lives in them and them in God. And so we know and rely on the love God has for us. - 1 John 4:13-16 (NIV)

God is love. Whoever lives in love lives in God, and God in them. This is how love is made complete among us so that we will have confidence on the day of judgment: In this world, we are like Jesus. There is no fear in love. But perfect love drives out fear because fear has to do with punishment. The one who fears is not made perfect in love. - 1 John 4:17-18 (NIV)

We love because he first loved us. Whoever claims to love God yet hates a brother or sister is a liar. For whoever does not love their brother and sister, whom they have seen, cannot love God, whom they have not seen. And he has given us this command: Anyone who loves God must also love their brother and sister. - 1 John 4:19-21 (NIV)

Day 2

The Greatest Commandment

In the old covenant, the emphasis was on keeping the laws of God, the law keeping was laborious and burdensome, and the law also brought with it the sense of judgment which I mentioned in yesterday's reading. God's grace is far more superior to the laws, and even though the people of Israel had to keep the law, provisions were also made by way of the blood sacrifices for their failures. When Jesus came to the earth, he became that perfect sacrifice that would put us in right standing once and for all with God once we come by way of the blood of Jesus. However, the knowledge of good and evil is embedded in our nature and the flesh will always try to puff up to prove that we can keep the law be it through discipline or self-will, and this system causes us to look to ourselves for the answer rather than resting in God's love for us.

The leaders of the law in Jesus' time had major issues with the gospel Jesus was preaching and always sought an opportunity to ridicule him. One day while Jesus was teaching in the temple courts the teachers of the law approached him to question his authority, but Jesus always had an answer ready that most time quieted and angered them all simultaneously. The question was posed to Jesus, "Of all the commandments, which is the most important?" (Mark 12:28 NIV). Jesus response was amazing, and every time I read it I must pause and drink in the depth of all that is contained within, "The most important one," answered Jesus, "is this: 'Hear, O Israel: The Lord our God, the Lord is one. Love the Lord your God with all your heart and with all your soul and with all your mind and with all your strength.' The second is this: 'Love your neighbor as yourself.' There is no commandment greater than these." (Mark 12:29-31 NIV).

Jesus summed up all the laws in the old covenant with just two and we translate those two laws in layman term as, "Love God; Love People." The truth about God is that he is love and he made us to love us not punish us. The bible tells us we are the object of his love, he created us to love us. Can you even fathom that thought, for me that was difficult to comprehend when all I had was heartache and rejection my whole life? Once I arrived at that place of understanding that no matter who rejected me or turned on me, God who is love made me just so he can love on me, oh that changed my life forever. The truth is we can never love God or people if we first don't know how much God loves us. I pray today you are gaining freedom from your past hurts and leaning in on the fact that God loves you.

Declaration: God loves me; God made me so He can pour out His love on me, God loves me!

DAILY SCRIPTURES FOR MEDITATION

One teacher of the law came and heard them debating. Noticing that Jesus had given them a good answer, he asked him, "Of all the commandments, which is the most important?"
"The most important one," answered Jesus, "is this: 'Hear, O Israel: The Lord our God, the Lord is one. Love the Lord your God with all your heart and with all your soul and with all your mind and with all your strength.' The second is this: 'Love your neighbor as yourself.' There is no commandment greater than these." - Mark 12:28-31 (NIV)

Yet the Lord set his affection on your ancestors and loved them, and he chose you, their descendants, above all the nations—as it is today. - Deuteronomy 10:15 (NIV)

How blessed is God! And what a blessing he is! He's the Father of our Master, Jesus Christ, and takes us to the high places of blessing in him. Long before he laid down earth's foundations, he had us in mind, had settled on us as the focus of his love, to be made whole and holy by his love. Long, long ago he decided to adopt us into his family through Jesus Christ. (What pleasure he took in planning this!) He wanted us to enter into the celebration of his lavish gift-giving by the hand of his beloved Son. - Ephesians 1:4-6 (MSG)

Day 3

God Is Seen Through Our Love

Today I would like to start by asking a simple question, "What draws you to someone you meet for the first time?" I don't think we give it much thought because we meet so many people in our lives occasionally but the common answer might be, "That person was so nice, so kind, so gracious, so welcoming, the smile was warm, or they had a sweet spirit." And this is how we describe people we are drawn too if they leave an impression on us. Well, this is how God said he would be known to the world and it will be through us. Jesus came to the earth to show forth the love of God to all humanity, but he also left his disciples with the same job description, "Go into all the world and preach the gospel to all creation." (Mark 16:15 NIV). In other words; do for the world what was done for you.

The Apostle John emphasizes that no one has ever seen God, but if we love one another then God lives in us, and that will cause others to have a glimpse of God. (1 John 4:12 NIV). The sad reality of the state of believers and that includes me is that we are always looking for something more complex and profound to do to make our lives better and we forget our primary purpose is to be a witness for Jesus, representing him to a lost and broken world in such desperate need of love. In Jesus's time, there was no shortage of rules, regulations and organized religion and the people were burdened, exhausted and defeated by it all. Jesus came to relieve us from the heavy burdens of trying to fix our lives and keeping all the rules, there was no time for healthy community and relationships. What the world needed was not more rules but a savior to set them free and Jesus was that savior. I am saved today because of the love of Jesus displayed through a disciple of Jesus who took time to pray for and with me, listen and was patient with me through the process. While Jesus did not show up in person, I saw God through the love the person showed me.

My friends, Jesus has done all that he can do to show his love, and he now wants to partner with you so his love can be made manifest to those around us. Sometimes we find it easier to preach to people about what they must do to get their lives right but according to the Apostle John, lives are changed when they encounter God and God is seen when people who don't know him see his children loving others, and that is the power of the gospel. John went so far to say, "Whoever claims to love God yet hates a brother or sister is a liar. For whoever does not love their brother and sister, whom they have seen, cannot love God, whom they have not seen" (1 John 4:20 NIV). The Apostle used strong, but necessary words and I pray that we will all aspire to love people the way God loves us.

Declaration: Today I will show love to everyone around me because I have received the love of God.

DAILY SCRIPTURES FOR MEDITATION

Whoever claims to love God yet hates a brother or sister is a liar. For whoever does not love their brother and sister, whom they have seen, cannot love God, whom they have not seen. And he has given us this command: Anyone who loves God must also love their brother and sister. - 1 John 4:20-21 (NIV)

A new command I give you: Love one another. As I have loved you, so you must love one another. - John 13:34 (NIV)

Day 4

Ahavah

In our culture, the word love is thrown around so freely and in the process loses its weight. We say things like, "I love that restaurant" or "I love that actor" or "I fell in love immediately, it was love at first sight." "I love that car or house." Love it seems has become so casual and is taken lightly. The way we use the word love, it suggests that love is temporary because when the next new thing or person comes around, we can forget the old and be in a new love relationship. Unfortunately, this is the world, but if you have been searching out a relationship with God, and the family of God you will understand that love is so much more than what is presented to us by our culture of the day.

In the Hebrew language, the word for love is "*Ahavah*, " and it is very beautiful in meaning. The root word for Ahavah is *ahav*, and it means, "*To give*," so it is understood as "I give" and "I love" (Bloomfield). Love is, therefore, more than a feeling; it is an action word as well and is accompanied with giving. Bloomfield also states, "Love is giving. Not only is love giving, but the actual process of giving develops the very connection between the giver and the receiver." I find the truth embedded in this statement to be revolutionary because we live in a world where technology while it has excellent benefits also has the power to work against us. We have found ourselves caught in the worldwide web with so many connections yet we are still so disconnected from human touch and face to face conversations. While we enjoy hundreds of friendships on social media, we do not understand those people, and we must go with what they show us on their profiles. We have watered down our relationships to texts communications only because face to face meeting will only draw down on our time and it will mean we must be involved and give some of our time and attention away.

"Giving is a condition that creates and sustains love. Without giving, there is no connection that is sustaining, and true relationships that are meaningful in our lives are those in which mutual giving take place" (Bloomfield).

From this statement we can see that no relationship will ever be sustained unless we will give and keep on giving to the people we are involved with. *Ahavah* is the love by which God lives and exist; it's a love that cannot be earned and it is a love that keeps on giving. In the Old Testament time and time again God showed his people *Ahavah*, he loved them unconditionally, and he asked that they show that love to others. Perhaps you are in a relationship today on rocky ground, I want to encourage you to start the change in your relationship by asking yourself, "How can I *Ahavah* this person in my life today, what can I give to them?"

Declaration: Today I will practice Ahavah (giving) to the people in my life.

DAILY SCRIPTURES FOR MEDITATION

The Lord did not set his affection on you and choose you because you were more numerous than other peoples, for you were the fewest of all peoples. But it was because the Lord loved you and kept the oath he swore to your ancestors he brought you out with a mighty hand and redeemed you from the land of slavery, from the power of Pharaoh king of Egypt. - Deuteronomy 7:7-8 (NIV)

The Lord appeared to us in the past, saying: "I have loved you with an everlasting love; I have drawn you with unfailing kindness. - Jeremiah 31:3 (NIV)

Because he loved your ancestors and chose their descendants after them, he brought you out of Egypt by his Presence and his great strength, - Deuteronomy 4:37 (NIV)

And now, Israel, what does the Lord your God ask of you but to fear the Lord your God, to walk in obedience to him, to love him, to serve the Lord your God with all your heart and with all your soul, and to observe the Lord's commands and decrees that I am giving you today for your own good? - Deuteronomy 10:12-13 (NIV)

"Do not seek revenge or bear a grudge against anyone among your people, but love your neighbor as yourself. I am the Lord. - Leviticus 19:18 (NIV)

Day 5

Greek Words For Love

There are quite a few words in the Greek language that describes the one word we use for love today, and I am very happy the Greek language can help us with the clarity which we so desperately need in this time when everyone loves everything. Today we will touch on four of those Greek words for insight and clarification.

1. **Eros** - A Greek and Roman god of love, often called the son of Aphrodite. He is better known by his Roman name Cupid. Note: The word erotic comes from the Greek word eros, which is the term for sexual love itself, as well as the god's name ("eros." Collins English Dictionary). Eros can also be described as the love of the body or romantic love (Ichykoo). From these definitions, we can see that Eros is a passionate and intense love that arouses romantic feelings and is merely emotional and sexual and while having an attraction is vital at the beginning of relationships it is not enough to sustain it long term without commitment and giving.

2. **Phileo** - refers to brotherly love and is most often exhibited in a close friendship. Best friends will display this generous and affectionate love for each other as each seeks to make the other happy - (www.gotquestions.org). This love was seen in the relationship between David and Jonathan - (1 Samuel 18: 1- 3). We have the choice when it comes to phileo because its relationships based on our likes and preferences.

3. **Storge** - is an affectionate love, the type of love one might have for family or a spouse. It is a naturally occurring, unforced type of love. Some examples of storge love can be found in the stories of Noah, Jacob, and siblings, Mary, Martha, and Lazarus. (www.gotquestions.org).

4. **Agape** - speaks of the most powerful, noblest type of love: sacrificial love. Agape love is more than a feeling—it is an act of the will. This is the love that God has for his people, and that prompted the sacrifice of his only Son, Jesus, for our sins. Jesus was agape love

personified. Christians are to love one another with agape love - (www.gotquestions.org). There is no greater love than agape for it is the God kind of love and this is the love God the Father shows to us. Agape is always accompanied with giving and doing, and here we see agape, and Ahavah is the same love that will sustain our relationship with God and others summing up the greatest commandments – Love God; Love People!

Declaration: I will aspire for the God kind of love to flow through me. Today I will function in Agape!

DAILY SCRIPTURES FOR MEDITATION

For God so loved the world that he gave his one and only Son, that whoever believes in him shall not perish but have eternal life. - John 3:16 (NIV)

Greater love has no one than this: to lay down one's life for one's friends. - John 15:13 (NIV)

If I speak in the tongues of men or of angels but do not have love, I am only a resounding gong or a clanging cymbal. If I have the gift of prophecy and can fathom all mysteries and all knowledge, and if I have a faith that can move mountains, but does not have love, I am nothing. If I give all I possess to the poor and give over my body to hardship that I may boast, but do not have love, I gain nothing. Love is patient; love is kind. It does not envy; it does not boast, it is not proud. It does not dishonor others; it is not self-seeking, it is not easily angered, it keeps no record of wrongs. Love does not delight in evil but rejoices with the truth. It always protects, always trusts, always hope, always perseveres. Love never fails.. And now these three remain faith, hope, and love. But the greatest of these is love. - 1 Corinthians 13:1-8a, 13(NIV)

Reflections

_____

_____

_____

_____

_____

_____

_____

_____

_____

_____

_____

_____

_____

_____

_____

_____

_____

_____

_____

_____

_____

_____

_____

_____

_____

Plan 11

PEACE IS YOUR INHERITANCE

==

In the busy world, we live in today; peace is valuable and more precious than silver or gold. Many are searching for peace in people and possessions- but real peace comes from Jesus. At the end of this plan, I trust you will gain a better understanding of the inheritance of peace that Christ left for you and embrace it in your daily life.

Day 1

Jesus Left You His Peace

In the Jewish culture, the people greet each other and say goodbye with the same word – Shalom! James Strong defines the word shalom in his concordance as, "Welfare, wholeness, health, prosperity, and peace." Wow! That seems like a mouthful from just a simple word as peace. As we look around in the world today, we see and hear of wars, fighting, murders, and weapons of mass destruction being constructed secretly. We are always bombarded with information about the wars in the Middle East more than any other nation in the world. Isn't it ironic that from this war-torn region their greetings and goodbyes speak of the one thing that is missing in their land which is the very Shalom of God?

In John chapter twelve Jesus is conversing with his disciples knowing the time of his death is quickly approaching. He offers comfort to them by letting them know though he is leaving, he will not leave them alone. I love how Jesus shows us the reality of this world but does not leave us hanging without hope. Jesus tells them of the impending dangers they will face after he is gone, but he also tells them the Holy Spirit will be given to them as a helper, comforter, and teacher in his place.

When someone knows their time to die is approaching they usually put things in place for their loved ones, they make a will, and they divide their inheritance among those they are leaving behind. They state their desires to be carried out after death. In this passage we see Jesus doing the same thing; he's preparing to leave the most valuable treasure he owned for his beloved disciples. One might think Jesus, being the Son of God would have given them silver and gold or a royal mansion. But to my surprise Jesus leaves in his will; his peace, his shalom.

Peace is vital and will determine the quality of life we live in this world. Often we believe more money, more possessions, more vacations, more social outings and more friends would bring us happiness and translate into peace in this chaotic world. But the truth is more stuff can never bring us true peace.

One of Jesus' titles is "Prince of Peace" – he is peace, peace belongs to him, and that is why only Jesus can give us real peace. In his conversation with this disciples, he said, "Peace I leave with you; My [own] peace I now give and bequeath to you." (John 14:27a AMP). The word "bequeath" means to leave or give personal property by will or to pass something to another; to hand down (Dictionary by Merriam Webster).

So of all the many qualities Jesus had he left for us the thing he saw we would need most in this world and it was not money or physical possession, but it was the peace by which he lived and operated while on earth. The world is searching for peace, but there is no real peace besides the Prince of peace. If you are a believer, then by right you have been given the peace which passes all understanding.

> *"When Christ died He left a will in which He gave His soul to His Father, His body to Joseph of Arimathea, His clothes to the soldiers, and His mother to John. But to His disciples, who had left all to follow Him, He left not silver or gold, but something far better - His PEACE!"* - Matthew Henry.

DAILY SCRIPTURES FOR MEDITATION

For to us, a child is born, to us, a son is given, and the government will be on his shoulders.
And he will be called Wonderful Counselor, Mighty God, Everlasting Father, Prince of Peace. - Isaiah 9:6 (NIV)

"I have told you these things, so that in me you may have peace. In this world, you will have trouble. But take heart! I have overcome the world." - John 16:33 (NIV)

But the Advocate, the Holy Spirit, whom the Father will send in my name, will teach you all things and will remind you of everything I have said to you. Peace I leave with you; my peace I give you. I do not give to you as the world gives. Do not let your hearts be troubled and do not be afraid. - John 14:26-27 (NIV)

Day 2

Peace Is Connected To Your Heart

According to the Strong's concordance the Hebrew word for heart is "leb, " and the Greek word is "kardia" it is the chief organ of physical life, and it occupies the most important place in the human system. The heart is also used figuratively as the inner man, the part of man which thinks, lives, has a personality and most of all respond to God. It is regarded as the seat of emotions like joy, fear or sorrow and is also referred to as the fountain of man's deeds.

The heart is significant to God because God said, "I will give you a new heart and put a new spirit in you; I will remove from you, your heart of stone and give you a heart of flesh." (Ezekiel 36:26 NIV). Most of what we go through in life are dealt with internally, our worries, our fears, and anxiety about the future or the unknown; we act out what is going on, on the inside. God gave us a new heart at the time of being born again, and now we must guard our hearts. The enemy knows that because of our relationship with Jesus, he cannot accuse us anymore before the Father, but it doesn't stop him from trying to steal our peace. He works overtime to ensure our lives are chaotic and confused all the time.

We live in a fast-paced world, everything seems to move at warped speed and time seems never to be enough. We are always in a hurry and still can never complete our tasks for the day. More families are getting disconnected; relationships are compromised and accumulating more seems always to be trending. Jesus knew the times we would be living in and provided us an inheritance of peace to carry us through.

Our heart functions best when we are at peace and as we established yesterday only Jesus could give us that peace. Even though we have an inheritance of peace, it can only be operative in our lives if we keep our hearts guarded. We must learn how to filter information going into our ear and eye gates because what we meditate on will eventually get into our hearts. We must come to the understanding that the world will only continue to move faster and get darker as the end approaches. Life will continue to be a rush, and we will face storms and obstacles, but we need not let the outward circumstances dictate our inner peace. As long as we stay heart connected to God's word his peace will surround us.

> *"If God be our God, He will give us peace in trouble. When there is a storm without, He will make peace within. The world can create trouble in peace, but God can create peace in trouble."* Thomas Watson

DAILY SCRIPTURES FOR MEDITATION

I will give you a new heart and put a new spirit in you; I will remove from you your heart of stone and give you a heart of flesh. - Ezekiel 36:26 (NIV)

Above all else, guard your heart, for everything you do flows from it. - Proverbs 4:23 (NIV)

But the Advocate, the Holy Spirit, whom the Father will send in my name, will teach you all things and will remind you of everything I have said to you. Peace I leave with you; my peace I give you. I do not give to you as the world gives. Do not let your hearts be troubled and do not be afraid. - John 14:26-27 (NIV)

Day 3

Peace Can Be Multiplied

When parents leave an inheritance for their children, I think it is with the hopes not only to take care but also to ensure they have a head start and advantage in life. They would hope to for their children to take what they have been given and multiply it. Jesus also left us with a peace that can be multiplied, how amazing is that? I find it exciting that the peace Jesus gave me will never run out but can go on perpetually. I have noticed as I walk and grow with the Lord the challenges of life continue, the obstacles seem more frequent, and the attacks intensify but, the more I stay planted and grounded in the words and promises of God I also recognize that I can better handle what comes my way.

Growing up in a single-parent home and then later on in an alcoholic home the one thing lacking was peace in the home and peace in my heart. I was plagued with chronic fear from an early age because I never knew what the nights would be like if my parent came home drunk. I would lay awake but pretend to be asleep in hopes to find that peace of heart. My life was tormented from the outside, and that translated to torment on the inside. The home was never happy, and fear ruled! I swore to myself that when I got out of that life, I would never allow myself or my children to experience a home like that.

More than anything in this world because of the life I experienced as a child, maintaining my inner peace is most important. I had to unlearn fear to receive love and be able to give my children what I never had. A happy home is my goal; I work hard for peace because I know what a lack of it can do to young children. I want you to know that a day at the spa or a shopping spree was not the answer to the years of torment I had gone through. I needed more than a getaway and a day at the spa. I needed truth to undo the lies and torment. So I dived deep into the word to discover who Jesus was and what he did for me and slowly my confidence grew in him, and every day I saw a new side of Jesus that is inexhaustible. I look back in hard times, and I see how faithful he was in bringing me through and that knowledge of his faithfulness strengthens me for the next trial, the next storm, the next obstacle. Our peace multiples when we grow in our understanding of who Jesus is.

"Peace is not the absence of trouble, but the presence of Christ." Sheila Walsh

DAILY SCRIPTURES FOR MEDITATION

Grace and peace be multiplied to you in the knowledge of God and of Jesus our Lord. - 2 Peter 1:2 (NKJV)

But the Advocate, the Holy Spirit, whom the Father will send in my name, will teach you all things and will remind you of everything I have said to you. Peace I leave with you; my peace I give you. I do not give to you as the world gives. Do not let your hearts be troubled and do not be afraid. - John 14:26-27 (NIV)

Day 4

Peace Produces Miracles

Our whole Christian walk should revolve around Jesus and most times we believe it is. We hear sermons about Jesus' miracles, we sing about the greatness of Jesus and nothing is wrong with sermons and worship that is Jesus centered. But, have you ever asked yourself, What caused Jesus to move and operate in such supernatural means even though he was always bombarded with both friends and enemies? The answer my friends is peace; he maintained and operated in such a level of peace there was no room for fear. Therefore, there were no limits to what he could do.

Jesus sleeps in the middle of an outrageous and to his disciples a life-threatening storm. When he is awoken from his sleep by Peter he is not frustrated, angry or upset, he merely speaks to the storm, and it stops immediately. (Mark 4:38 – 29 NIV)

Jesus feeds a multitude of people from only five loaves and two fish. (Mark 6:41 NIV). I get a panic attack just planning a birthday party for my children; I would have probably passed out from a just looking at the multitude.

Jesus raised Lazarus from the dead after he had been in the tomb for four days all the while maintaining his composure and continuing his ministry during the four days until he could get to Lazarus. (John 11:4 – 6 NIV)

Jesus turned ordinary drinking water into wine to save a wedding (John 2:1 – 11 NIV)

Jesus pays taxes to Caesar by sending Peter to open the mouth of a fish where the money would be found. (Matthew 17:24 – 27 NIV)

These are just a few miracles Jesus performed while he was on earth and He even promised that we would do things greater than he did. The reality of daily issues presented itself in Jesus' life, but at every juncture and every obstacle, Jesus ruled the situation with peace. So often we lose sleep over situations that only Jesus can handle, we worry about provisions, sickness, and disease. We are anxious about being embarrassed if we can't keep up with our friends and culture and about having enough. Well, today I want to encourage you to give over to Jesus all that you have no control of and everything that is bigger than you and rest in him, rest in his love for you knowing he is able. Just think about this, the very peace that Jesus operated in and performed all these miracles is the very same peace he left for you!

> *"Christ's miracles were not the suspension of the natural order but the restoration of the natural order. They were a reminder of what once was prior to the fall and a preview of what will eventually be a universal reality once again--a world of peace and justice, without death, disease, or conflict."* Tim Keller

DAILY SCRIPTURES FOR MEDITATION

Jesus was in the stern, sleeping on a cushion. The disciples woke him and said to him, "Teacher, don't you care if we drown?" He got up, rebuked the wind and said to the waves, "Quiet! Be still!" Then the wind died down, and it was completely calm. - Mark 4:38-39 (NIV)

Taking the five loaves and the two fish and looking up to heaven, he gave thanks and broke the loaves. Then he gave them to his disciples to distribute to the people. He also divided the two fish among them all. They all ate and were satisfied, and the disciples picked up twelve basketfuls of broken pieces of bread and fish. - Mark 6:41-43 (NIV)

When he heard this, Jesus said, "This sickness will not end in death. No, it is for God's glory so that God's Son may be glorified through it. "Now Jesus loved Martha and her sister and Lazarus. - John 11:4-16 (NIV)

Jesus, once more deeply moved, came to the tomb. It was a cave with a stone laid across the entrance. "Take away the stone," he said. "But, Lord," said Martha, the sister of the dead man, "by this time there is a bad odor, for he has been there four days." Then Jesus said, "Did I not tell you that if you believe, you will see the glory of God?" So they took away the stone. Then Jesus looked up and said, "Father, I thank you that you have heard me. I knew that you always hear me, but I said this for the benefit of the people standing here, that they may believe that you sent me." When he had said this, Jesus called in a loud voice, "Lazarus, come out!" The dead man came out, his hands and feet wrapped with strips of linen and a cloth around his face. Jesus said to them, "Take off the grave clothes and let him go." - John 11:38-44 (NIV)

After Jesus and his disciples arrived in Capernaum, the collectors of the two-drachma temple tax came to Peter and asked, "Doesn't your teacher pay the temple tax?" "Yes, he does," he replied.
When Peter came into the house, Jesus was the first to speak. "What do you think, Simon?" he asked. "From whom do the kings of the earth collect duty and taxes—from their own children or from others?" "From others," Peter answered. "Then the children are exempt," Jesus said to him. "But so that we may not cause offense, go to the lake and throw out your line. Take the first fish you catch; open its mouth, and you will find a four-drachma coin. Take it and give it to them for my tax and yours." - Matthew 17:24-27 (NIV)

But the Advocate, the Holy Spirit, whom the Father will send in my name, will teach you all things and will remind you of everything I have said to you. Peace I leave with you; my peace I give you. I do not give to you as the world gives. Do not let your hearts be troubled and do not be afraid. - John 14:26-27 (NIV)

Day 5

Peace Keeps The Miracle

In the book of Mark, there is a very familiar story of the woman with an issue of blood. This woman had suffered for twelve years searching out doctor after doctor with no signs of relief. Every day she was becoming weaker and losing life, she was embarrassed and outcast because of the laws of her day. Her situation would be deemed as impossible, hopeless and beyond repair. Her issue had not only made her weak, but she ran low in finances, she was in dire straits and in need of a miracle. The story tells us she heard reports of Jesus and the supernatural miracles happening in the community. Her faith grew, and a glimmer of hope was sparked deep within. Only the Prince of Peace could cause faith to arise in the heart of the hopeless and desperate.

She heard Jesus would be passing by her and she pressed through the crowd to touch the healer, and she succeeded. As she touched Jesus' garment, she was immediately healed, and this drawing down of power from Jesus caused him to stop to discover who had touched him. The woman was afraid and came forth to show herself, and at this point Jesus spoke these powerful words," And he said to her, Daughter, your faith (your trust and confidence in Me, springing from faith in God) has restored you to health. Go in (into) peace and be continually healed and freed from your [distressing bodily] disease." (Mark 5:34)(AMPC)

Jesus said her faith caused a miracle of healing, but then he said, "Go in (into) peace and be continually healed and freed from your [distressing bodily] disease." The word *into* in the Greek is *"en, "* and it means to *step into* (Dictionary by Vines). For example, step into a house, so Jesus implied that for her to keep the miracle of healing, she would have to now step into the realm or place of perpetual peace, inner peace. Often we receive divine healing at a prayer meeting, worship service or miracle crusade. We feel the healing touch of God, but once we leave the atmosphere of God's presence we forget, and trials and troubles of everyday life rob us of the miracle. The grace of God gives us everything freely, but the peace of God keeps all that God gives. Inner peace is equal to a happy life;

inner peace is not dictated by outward circumstances but by knowing and operating in the inheritance we received from the Prince of Peace.

"A great many people are trying to make peace, but that has already been done. God has not left it for us to do; all we have to do – is to enter into it." Dwight L Moody

DAILY SCRIPTURES FOR MEDITATION

And there was a woman who had had a flow of blood for twelve years, and who had endured much suffering under [the hands of] many physicians and had spent all that she had, and was no better but instead grew worse. She had heard the reports concerning Jesus, and she came up behind Him in the throng and touched His garment, for she kept saying, If I only touch His garments, I shall be restored to health. And immediately her flow of blood was dried up at the source, and [suddenly] she felt in her body that she was healed of her [distressing] ailment. And Jesus, recognizing in Himself that the power proceeding from Him had gone forth, turned around immediately in the crowd and said, who touched My clothes? And the disciples kept saying to Him, you see the crowd pressing hard around You from all sides, and you ask, Who touched Me? Still, He kept looking around to see her who had done it. But the woman, knowing what had been done for her, though alarmed and frightened and trembling, fell down before Him and told Him the whole truth. And He said to her, Daughter, your faith (your trust and confidence in Me, springing from faith in God) has restored you to health. Go in (into) peace and be continually healed and freed from your [distressing bodily] disease. - Mark 5:25-34 (AMPC)

But the Advocate, the Holy Spirit, whom the Father will send in my name, will teach you all things and will remind you of everything I have said to you. Peace I leave with you; my peace I give you. I do not give to you as the world gives. Do not let your hearts be troubled and do not be afraid. - John 14:26-27 (NIV)

Day 6

Prayer of Peace

Father, today I want to just thank you for the revelation I received during these past five days. I want to ask you to forgive me for running for the temporary peace the world offers. I stand before you today knowing the inheritance Jesus left me is priceless and beyond comparison to any material possessions. Holy Spirit, teach me how to activate and use my inheritance of peace, show me what I must root out of my heart so I can create space to cultivate a peaceful heart. Open my eyes to see Jesus in the scriptures I read every day, so I can grow in my knowledge of his greatness, faithfulness, and his character.

I want the inheritance of peace to be multiplied many times over in my life. Holy Spirit, help me to operate in the measure of peace that Jesus operated in so I may see countless miracles in my life and those around me, let fear, anxiety, and worry have no room in my life for the peace of God expands in and around me. Holy Spirit, please give me the wisdom, strength, and courage to enter the realm of the peace of God so all the blessings so freely given may be kept. Let my life be an example for those around me to see your glory. I thank you for hearing my prayer, and I believe peace is my inheritance. Amen.

"All the glory and beauty of Christ are manifested within, and there He delights to dwell; His visits there are frequent, His condescension amazing, His conversation sweet, His comforts refreshing; and the peace that He brings passeth all understanding." Thomas Kempis

DAILY SCRIPTURES FOR MEDITATION

Do not be anxious about anything, but in every situation, by prayer and petition, with thanksgiving, present your requests to God. 7 And the peace of God, which transcends all understanding, will guard your hearts and your minds in Christ Jesus. - Philippians 4:6-7 (NIV)

But the Advocate, the Holy Spirit, whom the Father will send in my name, will teach you all things and will remind you of everything I have said to you. Peace I leave with you; my peace I give you. I do not give to you as the world gives. Do not let your hearts be troubled and do not be afraid. - John 14:26-27 (NIV)

Reflections

_____

_____

_____

_____

_____

_____

_____

_____

_____

_____

_____

_____

_____

_____

_____

_____

_____

_____

_____

_____

_____

_____

_____

_____

_____

Plan 12

PURSUING GOD'S REST

==

In the world, we live in today, "rest" seems like a foreign word to many of us. We all have so much to deal with, and without proper rest, the door is open for stress to plant its ugly feet and wreak havoc in our lives. But the good news is, God designed rest and it's only in pursuing his presence that true rest can be found.

Day 1

Pursuing God's Rest

Often when we think about resting, we have this idea that we are laying down, doing absolutely nothing and being fast asleep. That had been my idea of rest most of my life, and today we live in a world where we must actually fight to find time to rest. But rest is so much more than just being asleep or being stationary. Rest has a lot to do with our inner man, often we lay down to sleep but suddenly we are awakened by a panic attack due to a dream, and once we are awake the thoughts of our future, finances, children, relationships, business or ministry bombard us. Mind you, we are in a resting position, but still, the inner man is at work. We can be sitting on a white sandy beach overlooking blue ocean waters and still not be at rest because thoughts, phone calls, and social media encroach at our doors competing for our attention. Long ago people worked hard during the day; an eight-hour shift and return home for dinner with the family around a table with some delightful conversations, probably catch TV together or pray together and then bed.

In these times money has become our god, and the body, soul, and spirit of man are disregarded and neglected to gain more, achieve more, and pursue more. Excessive material possessions have ruined the sanctity of family and marriage. We work longer and harder, and even though the money may be coming in, we stand to lose much more like our health, the chance of making memories, and recreation time to enjoy all that God has given us. God has designed us to work, but he also created us for rest.

God lives by the principle of rest, and we see this principle while he was creating the earth, the bible tells us that "On the seventh day God rested" (Genesis 2:2 NIV). God considers rest holy that's how serious this topic of rest is. Long before God gave the laws to the Israelites, God declared the Sabbath as holy and necessary. God later commanded his people to celebrate the Sabbath as a lasting covenant between him and them. (Exodus 31:16)

God is the designer of all creation, and he knows what we need better than we do. God knew the earth, the soil, the trees, the birds, the fish, the cattle and all other creation would need rest. Giving up one day out of seven days to the Lord is a sign we trust him as our provider, and we rely on him to sustain us and not our own strength. God is about rest, and he said because the children of Israel were disobedient in the wilderness and because they refused to believe him, they will not enter his rest. (Psalm 95:10 – 11)

As we look across the globe many diseases are arising, people are suffering from hypertension, anxiety, and fear and the medical field is working tirelessly to find cures for them all. Perhaps if we pursued the rest of God the way we seek money and material stuff, we might find the cure we are looking for. Let us pursue God's rest today!

DAILY SCRIPTURES FOR MEDITATION

By the seventh day God had finished the work he had been doing; so on the seventh day, he rested from all his work. Then God blessed the seventh day and made it holy because on it he rested from all the work of creating that he had done. – Genesis 2:2-3 (NIV)

Remember the Sabbath day by keeping it holy. Six days you shall labor and do all your work, but the seventh day is a Sabbath to the Lord your God. On it you shall not do any work, neither you, nor your son or daughter, nor your male or female servant, nor your animals, nor any foreigner residing in your towns. - Exodus 20:8-10 (NIV)

Six days do your work, but on the seventh day do not work, so that your ox and your donkey may rest, and so that the slave born in your household and the foreigner living among you may be refreshed. - Exodus 23:12 (NIV)

Day 2

Rest Requires Faith

Now that sounds very strange; rest requires faith! I would think to lie down and watch a movie or just relaxing requires nothing. But when you look around you there seems to be a race against time, people including myself are scurrying around trying to meet deadlines and trying to put in thirty hours of working into a ten hour or longer day.

The mind of man is set on achieving more, being on the cutting edge of their field, and the quest to bring out the next new thing. It is incredible how we get so tired and bored with our creations so quickly, and that invokes the cycle of getting something new every week, season, or year, yet the creation of God is still sustained and enjoyed six thousand years later. Now I am not against staying on the cutting edge of our fields, or creating and discovering new treatments, technology, systems and strategies to make life easier and better; but when these things take precedence over time spent with our Creator, families, and friends and church we are bordering on a breakdown sooner or later.

I've looked at the Jewish people for years as I live near a Jewish neighborhood and I am stunned at the ridiculous visible blessings upon their lives even though they have been such a persecuted people. Everything they seem to put their hands to become blessed and prosper, and yet they close their businesses on what we would consider the busiest shopping day of the week which is Saturday. They shut down everything, and they observe the Sabbath, a Holy day of rest unto the Lord. They walk to the synagogues with their families, and they focus that day on their God, doing no work. Won't you say this takes real faith to enjoy the busiest business day off from work and rest in the Lord? It sure does.

While we are not under the old covenant law but the new covenant grace, we miss the point that God instituted rest from the very creation of the earth. While we may not observe the Saturday Sabbath like the Jews, the principle of rest remains an essential aspect of life for all peoples. We may go to church on Sundays, but still we leave our businesses open, and we compromise our rest in the Lord by trying to do more hoping that someday we won't have to work so hard, but that is a lie from the devil because the more we work now, the less time we have left with to enjoy life.

The children of Israel had to learn how important the Sabbath was the tough way. They refused to rest the land every seven years as God had commanded them. For four hundred and ninety years they ignored God and never let their animals and land rest and as a result for all the Sabbaths missed they spent a year in bondage, they were carried away into captivity having to leave their land so it could rest as God commanded. Seventy years was spent in captivity due to their disobedience.

Well, you might argue today we are not under that law, but the fact remains that God designed us for rest and if we don't make the time to rest in him, drinking in the goodness of his word, soaking in the anointing of his presence we too can find ourselves in captivity to sickness, disease, anxiety, fear, and frustrations. Our bodies are designed for rest, and when we don't give it rest, it will take it. Let's not be stubborn and have to learn this lesson the hard way. Have faith in God and rest!

DAILY SCRIPTURES FOR MEDITATION

Therefore, since the promise of entering his rest still stands, let us be careful that none of you be found to have fallen short of it. For we also have had the good news proclaimed to us, just as they did; but the message they heard was of no value to them, because they did not share the faith of those who obeyed. - Hebrews 4:1-2 (NIV)

"He carried into exile to Babylon the remnant, who escaped from the sword, and they became servants to him and his successors until the kingdom of Persia came to power. The land enjoyed its Sabbath rests; all the time of its desolation it rested until the seventy years were completed in fulfillment of the word of the Lord spoken by Jeremiah." - 2 Chronicles 36:20-21 (NIV)

There remains, then, a Sabbath-rest for the people of God; for anyone who enters God's rest also rests from their works, just as God did from his. Let us, therefore, make every effort to enter that rest, so that no one will perish by following their example of disobedience. -

Hebrews 4:9-11 (NIV)

You may ask, "What will we eat in the seventh year if we do not plant or harvest our crops?" I will send you such a blessing in the sixth year that the land will yield enough for three years. While you plant during the eighth year, you will eat from the old crop and will continue to eat from it until the harvest of the ninth year comes in. - Leviticus 25:20-22 (NIV)

Day 3

Your Promise From God Will Manifest As You Rest In Him

Words and promises from humankind in the world prove very fickle. People change their minds quickly, today people will love you, tomorrow they may hate you and so living our lives based on the promises of men is a big set up for failure and disappointments. One thing we can rest in is the Word of God, he is good on his promises, and he never disappoints. I have learned to trust God's Word more and more as I grow in my knowledge of him and I teach others to lean on his words and not man's. God seems to love to work in cycles, and one of the prominent cycles we observe in the Bible is cycles of sevens; seven days in a week, seven-year Sabbaths, seventy years of captivity, etc. Doctors observe this seven cycle, they usually say, "A virus will run its course in seven days," I guess God loves the number seven and I am happy with that.

I love searching out the scriptures for God's promises and staying on them until I see God move to answer those promises. One promise I love in the Bible is, "I have found your word, and it is health and healing to all my flesh" (Proverbs 4:22 NIV). And in the book of Isaiah God specifically, talks about the blessings one will enjoy if they consider resting as *Holy*. (Isaiah 58: 13- 14)

Even as I am writing this plan, I am in a place of forced rest due to an inflamed inner ear, as a wife, mom, pastor, author and teacher I find it hard to rest. I actually feel guilty when I take moments of rest because I was tricked into believing I am wasting time when I rest. But being sick for the past couple of weeks has brought to my attention I may be disobedient to observing the Holy day of rest. Sickness is one way the body will take rest, but it is not the healthy way. Our bodies will give us signs and warnings to slow down but guess what? We never listen until it is too late and we are forced to rest. "Stress doesn't only make us feel awful emotionally. It can also exacerbate just about any health condition you can think of." Says Jay Winner, MD. Wow! Now that's scary.

They also listed 10 health problems related to stress:

- Heart disease

- Asthma

- Obesity

- Diabetes

- Headaches

- Depression and anxiety

- Gastrointestinal problems

- Alzheimer's disease

- Accelerated aging

- Premature death.

This information is staggering and if we do not see the need to stop, breathe and rest we are opening ourselves up to greater risk. God is showing us more and more that we can work but we must trust him to take care of us while we rest in him.

DAILY SCRIPTURES FOR MEDITATION

As the rain and the snow come down from heaven, and do not return to it without watering the earth and making it bud and flourish, so that it yields seed for the sower and bread for the eater, so is my word that goes out from my mouth: It will not return to me empty, but will accomplish what I desire and achieve the purpose for which I sent it. Isaiah 55:10-11 (NIV)

Be not wise in your own eyes; reverently fear and worship the Lord and turn [entirely] away from evil.
It shall be health to your nerves and sinews, and marrow and moistening to your bones. - Proverbs 3:7-8 (AMPC)

Day 4

Rest Destroys Stress

Jesus came to be our savior! This we know, but save us from what? He came to save us from eternal separation from God the Father because keeping all the laws of God was impossible. The people were tired, frustrated and burdened by the law and Jesus came to free them from this burden. To be work conscious leaves little room for God or rest consciousness and that opens the door wide for stress to enter in, because now instead of enlisting the help of God we have the whole burden of making our plans work on our limited wisdom and knowledge.

We can see God's heart throughout the scriptures for rest for his people. He prepared a beautiful garden for Adam and Eve to take care of (work) and in the cool of the day God came down and fellowshipped with them (rest). (Genesis 2:2 NIV). God took the Israelites out of Egypt (hard work) to the wilderness with hopes to take them into Canaan, a place prepared for them (rest). It has always been God's heart for his people to find rest in the midst of all the work.

Jimmy Winner, M.D says, "Stress isn't just in your head" It's a built in-physiologic response to a threat. When you're stressed your body responds. Your blood vessels constrict. Your blood pressure and pulse rise. You breathe faster. Your bloodstream is flooded with hormones such as cortisol and adrenaline. When you're chronically stressed, those physiologic changes, over time, can lead to health problems."

There are many benefits to rest, and I pray that we will all seek God to pursue his rest. Here are just a few benefits of rest:

- Gives time for energy levels to return

- Give time to contemplate problems

- The body can save energy during rest

- Produce more in less time – (Frederick Taylor a management consultant sought to improve industrial efficiency through rest)

In Dr. Caroline Leaf's book, Who Switched off My Brain, she states:

> "If you don't build relaxation into your lifestyle you will become a less effective thinker, defeating your ability to accomplish the mental tasks that stole your relaxation in the first place. In fact, for the brain to function like it should, it needs to regroup/consolidation time. If it doesn't get this, it will send out signals in the form of high-level stress hormones, some of which are epinephrine, norepinephrine, and cortisol. If these chemicals constantly flow, they create a "white noise" effect that increases anxiety and blocks clear thinking and the processing of information."

I know it's hard to grasp the thought that if I rest, I can produce more but that is the amazing supernatural work of God at work when we adhere to his principles. I pray you would weigh what hangs in the balance for your future, your health, your family and your very own life and today I declare you will pursue God's rest!

DAILY SCRIPTURES FOR MEDITATION

Six days do your work, but on the seventh day do not work, so that your ox and your donkey may rest, and so that the slave born in your household and the foreigner living among you may be refreshed. - Exodus 23:12 (NIV)

On the day the Lord gives you relief from your suffering and turmoil and from the harsh labor forced on you, you will take up this taunt against the king of Babylon: How the oppressor has come to an end! How his fury has ended! - Isaiah 14:3-4 (NIV)

This is what the Lord says: "Stand at the crossroads and look; ask for the ancient paths, ask where the good way is, and walk in it, and you will find rest for your souls. But you said, 'We will not walk in it.' - Jeremiah 6:16 (NIV)

Then, because so many people were coming and going that they did not even have a chance to eat, he said to them, "Come with me by yourselves to a quiet place and get some rest." - Mark 6:31 (NIV)

Do not be anxious about anything, but in every situation, by prayer and petition, with thanksgiving, present your requests to God. And the peace of God, which transcends all understanding, will guard your hearts and your minds in Christ Jesus. - Philippians 4:6-7 (NIV)

"Come to me, all you who are weary and burdened, and I will give you rest. Take my yoke upon you and learn from me, for I am gentle and humble in heart, and you will find rest for your souls. - Matthew 11:28-29 (NIV)

Then I heard a voice from heaven say, "Write this: Blessed are the dead who die in the Lord from now on." "Yes," says the Spirit, "they will rest from their labor, for their deeds will follow them." - Revelation 14:13(NIV)

Reflections

_____

_____

_____

_____

_____

_____

_____

_____

_____

_____

_____

_____

_____

_____

_____

_____

_____

_____

_____

_____

_____

_____

_____

_____

_____

Plan 13

TAKE THE HELP

==

We all go thru life running on self-effort, and we eventually get to the *"pulling out our hair"* moments from all that we must deal with daily. However, did you know that our Heavenly Father gave us a helper? This helper supersedes all our natural abilities and once we get to the point of total dependence life becomes easier- *"Would you take the help today?"*

Day 1

You Have Help From The Holy Spirit

Every day we wake is a gift from God, but with every day comes challenges, struggles, dead ends, frustrations, anxiety, and fear, this is just to list a few things we face daily. It seems we are a people desperately needing help, wouldn't you agree? Jesus was acutely aware we would need all the help we can get, and he promises to give us a helper. The world has caught on to the fact that everyone needs help and every day we are bombarded with tips, tricks, DIY videos, books, magazines, TV shows all offering the answer to our every need. But, somehow these solutions seem to fall short, and soon we are searching for the next best thing to help us. I have been on the end of this especially in wanting a quick fix to lose weight; I know many of you can identify with this very plight. I have tried many pills, diets, workout plans, and strategies but to no avail. I always end up disappointed and looking for the next quick fix. It's like a cycle, and I convince myself this time this product will work, or this time I will be more disciplined, or this time I will get the help I need.

If you have been caught in this cycle of failure, I want to encourage you not to give up because you have been given the best help on planet earth and the wonderful thing is this help is not a thing, product or strategy but he is a person. He is the third person of the God-head; he is the Holy Spirit. Most of my life I never understood the Holy Spirit, I was spooked by him because of the many reactions from people in church when they spoke about the Holy Spirit coming and manifesting in corporate meetings. Because of human reactions, I wanted little to do with this Holy Spirit and as you can guess I lived life in a cycle of failure.

As I began pastoring, I soon realized I could not adequately minister to others without the help of the Holy Spirit. My sermons were dry, I had no heart connection to the people, I came home after every service feeling empty, and after a while, I cried out in prayer to the Lord, and he spoke to my heart, he said, "Take the help." It has been a journey of many ups and downs but through it all, I am comforted by the truth I have a Helper, and I never have to go it alone. Well perhaps you are thinking the Holy Spirit will only help those who are in ministry, but that is not true, the Holy Spirit is our Helper period. He is available to all who believe in Jesus Christ, and he will never leave us, and no matter what area you are struggling in the Helper holds the answer. Will you take the help today?

Holy Spirit I want to know more about you and I need your help!

DAILY SCRIPTURES FOR MEDITATION

And I will ask the Father, and He will give you another Comforter (Counselor, Helper, Intercessor, Advocate, Strengthener, and Standby), that He may remain with you forever— The Spirit of Truth, Whom the world cannot receive (welcome, take to its heart), because it does not see Him or know and recognize Him. But you know and recognize Him, for He lives with you [constantly] and will be in you. - John 14:16-17 (AMPC)

However, I am telling you nothing but the truth when I say it is profitable (good, expedient, advantageous) for you that I go away. Because if I do not go away, the Comforter (Counselor, Helper, Advocate, Intercessor, Strengthener, Standby) will not come to you [into close fellowship with you]; but if I go away, I will send Him to you [to be in close fellowship with you]. - John 16:7 (AMPC)

Day 2

He Transforms And Equips Us

The life I lived before I came to Jesus Christ was one of self-satisfaction; my way or the highway! I had no present father in my life so growing up without love expressed made me very callous, hard, rebellious and prideful. I couldn't take advice because I thought I knew it all; it only led me down a road of multiple mistakes, heartbreak, and a stony heart. Perhaps your situation differs from mine, but I am sure you have experienced some things in life that caused your heart to become hard also.

The beauty of the Holy Spirit is his eagerness to enter our lives even though we are messed up, cold towards life, imperfect and unlovable. In the world, if someone does not have the Holy Spirit working in their lives, there is no way they would be eager to embrace the chaos of another person's life, but instead they would look for ways to avoid a person that's unworthy of their time and effort. Trying to live this life without the help of the Holy Spirit only leads us to failure and frustrations.

Jesus was getting ready to leave the earth, and the disciples were worried knowing the persecution about to be unleashed. Jesus said, "And I will ask the Father, and he will give you another Comforter (Counselor, Helper, Intercessor, Advocate, Strengthener, and Standby," that he may remain with you forever." (John 14:16 AMP). In other words, Jesus was saying, "In order to deal with life you would need help from someone that is just like me." And as promised on the day of Pentecost the Holy Spirit came like a rushing wind. (Acts 2:2 NIV). Do you see the description, rushing; it suggests an eagerness to come and be part of our lives. The Holy Spirit hasn't changed his excitement or enthusiasm for indwelling a born-again Christian. As long as we accept Christ as our Savior, the Holy Spirit is waiting with great anticipation for a life that can be transformed.

To be free from a past of abuse, rejection or shame or to forgive those who have hurt you, or to break an addiction, anger or hate we must take the help of the promised Holy Spirit. To face life challenges like battling sickness and disease, or coping with losing a job or house or loved one we just don't have that strength on our own. It is my prayer for you today that you could recognize you cannot do this life anymore without the Help of the Holy Spirit and allow him to have free reign in your life so you may be transformed and equipped for what lies ahead.

Holy Spirit please be more active in my life, please transform and equip me for life.

DAILY SCRIPTURES FOR MEDITATION

And I will ask the Father, and He will give you another Comforter (Counselor, Helper, Intercessor, Advocate, Strengthener, and Standby), that He may remain with you forever. - John 14:16 (AMPC)

And when the day of Pentecost had fully come, they were all assembled in one place, when suddenly there came a sound from heaven like the rushing of a violent tempest blast, and it filled the whole house in which they were sitting. And there appeared to them tongues resembling fire, which were separated and distributed and which settled on each one of them. And they were all filled (diffused throughout their souls) with the Holy Spirit and began to speak in other (different, foreign) languages (tongues), as the Spirit kept giving them clear and loud expression [in each tongue in appropriate words]. - Acts 2:1-4 (AMPC)

And such some of you were [once]. But you were washed clean (purified by a complete atonement for sin and made free from the guilt of sin), and you were consecrated (set apart, hallowed), and you were justified [pronounced righteous, by trusting] in the name of the Lord Jesus Christ and in the [Holy] Spirit of our God. - 1 Corinthians 6:11 (AMPC)

Day 3

He Helps Us Lead Godly Lives

With so much access to the world through technology, our desires are satisfied in real time. Long ago one had to think long and hard of how to satisfy the lust of the eyes and flesh. Pornography was not as accessible as it is today, one can be exposed to indecent images by just scrolling your social media pages. People can feed their lusts from the privacy of their bedrooms, and no one will know. The dress code of our culture leaves nothing to the imagination when all our body parts are bared for all to see. I remember a time when watching a kissing scene on TV with my mom in the room would cause shame to arise in me and cause me to look away. Now, our billboards and commercials expose so much more to feed the eyes that shame and embarrassment is a thing of the past. We can now feed our soul with runway shows of lingerie models and have no qualms about it because in today's world less is actually more. I know this scenario sounds extreme but the truth is this is the world, and if we do not have the help needed, we too can fall prey to the devil's schemes.

To combat the sinful desires that still seek to raise its head in our lives, we must have a mind stayed on Christ and his word. When images are being launched at us from every side, we must have an antidote for it. The Holy Spirit helps us to remember the scriptures we read every day if we ask him. Once we read the word, we must spend time meditating on it, going over it, speaking it. Through this process, it gets lodged in our memory, so when evil arises we can call on the Holy Spirit, and he will bring back to our memory everything needed at that moment to overcome the desires, not of him. This life we live must now be lived with the Helper in mind, being conscious that he is there every minute of the day and he never leaves.

Once the seed of Christ is deposited in us, we now must nourish that seed by reading the word, meditating on the word, speaking the word and hiding the word in our hearts. As we practice the word, the Spirit bears fruit in our lives, and we can overcome hate with love, chaos with peace, tribulation with patience, trials with joy, rudeness with kindness and so on. I know everyone wants a quick fix, and so do I. Often I think about Jesus leaving the earth and perhaps he could have just raptured the disciples with him. But the Holy Spirit had to come so simple, imperfect people like us could be saved, cleansed, transformed and be witnesses of God's great love. Let us try to enlist the help of the Holy Spirit today, to meditate on the word of God and hide it in our hearts so the fruit of him will have room to bloom in our lives.

Holy Spirit, please help me to remember what I read from your word so I may overcome the evil of my day.

DAILY SCRIPTURES FOR MEDITATION

And I will ask the Father, and He will give you another Comforter (Counselor, Helper, Intercessor, Advocate, Strengthener, and Standby), that He may remain with you forever - John 14:16 (AMPC)

This Book of the Law shall not depart out of your mouth, but you shall meditate on it day and night, that you may observe and do according to all that is written in it. For then you shall make your way prosperous, and then you shall deal wisely and have good success. - Joshua 1:8 (AMPC)

But the Comforter (Counselor, Helper, Intercessor, Advocate, Strengthener, Standby), the Holy Spirit, Whom the Father will send in My name [in My place, to represent Me and act on My behalf], He will teach you all things. And He will cause you to recall (will remind you of, bring to your remembrance) everything I have told you. - John 14:26 (AMPC)

But the fruit of the [Holy] Spirit [the work which His presence within accomplishes] is love, joy (gladness), peace, patience (an even temper, forbearance), kindness, goodness (benevolence), faithfulness, Gentleness (meekness, humility), self-control (self-restraint, continence). Against such things, there is no law [that can bring a charge]. - Galatians 5:22-23 (AMPC)

Day 4

He Helps Us Pray

Having a prayer life is essential and before we even learn how to read and meditate on God's word I think we all know how to utter a prayer to God. People pray all the time for blessings, breakthroughs, open doors, favor, good health and the keeping of our families. But I am sure sometimes, you believed you prayed hard and long, and the answer never came the way you prayed. Or perhaps you have been in a place where the situation was so bad you did not even have the words to pray. I have been on both sides of these prayers, and during those times I believed God failed me and if you are honest I am sure you have also felt that way.

As you grow in your relationship with the Holy Spirit becoming more aware of his presence and fellowshipping with him, you realize that praying is so much more than asking for blessings for yourself and your family but prayer actually becomes the bridge for God's heart to be known in the earth. As a Pastor it can become overwhelming with prayer requests flowing in from our media ministry, local church, praying for the community, the country, nations and individual needs. Only helped by the Holy Spirit could all these prayers be made known. The Holy Spirit knows what the will of God is for our lives, did you get that? he knows the will of God, and he also knows what is in our hearts. Sometimes what is in our hearts is not always the will that God has for us, and those are the times we might not have received the answer we were hoping for.

Over the years I have learnt how to yield myself to the Holy Spirit saying something like this, "Holy Spirit, I don't know exactly what the will of God is here, and I am not sure my desire is his right now, but I yield myself to you, and I ask you to help me pray your will in this situation." It is that simple, and then there are times I try praying for someone or something, and I don't have the words, and in those times I prayed in the spirit using my heavenly tongue. In that way, I know the Holy Spirit is praying through me for the will of God which I could never have known by my flesh.

Maybe you are at this place of not knowing the will of God for a particular situation, and you have run out of words, I want to encourage you to yield your heart and mind to the Holy Spirit and ask him to help you pray your will today.

Holy Spirit I need your help to pray for my life today.

DAILY SCRIPTURES FOR MEDITATION

And I will ask the Father, and He will give you another Comforter (Counselor, Helper, Intercessor, Advocate, Strengthener, and Standby), that He may remain with you forever. - John 14:16 (AMPC)

Pray, therefore, like this: Our Father Who is in heaven, hallowed (kept holy) be Your name. Your kingdom come, Your will be done on earth as it is in heaven. - Matthew 6:9-10 (AMPC)

So too the [Holy] Spirit comes to our aid and bears us up in our weakness; for we do not know what prayer to offer nor how to offer it worthily as we ought, but the Spirit Himself goes to meet our supplication and pleads in our behalf with unspeakable yearnings and groanings too deep for utterance. And He Who searches the hearts of men knows what is in the mind of the [Holy] Spirit [what His intent is], because the Spirit intercedes and pleads [before God] in behalf of the saints according to and in harmony with God's will. - Romans 8:26-27 (AMPC)

Do not fret or have any anxiety about anything, but in every circumstance and in everything, by prayer and petition (definite requests), with thanksgiving, continue to make your wants known to God. And God's peace [shall be yours, that tranquil state of a soul assured of its salvation through Christ, and so fearing nothing from God and being content with its earthly lot of whatever sort that is, that peace] which transcends all understanding shall garrison and mount guard over your hearts and minds in Christ Jesus. For the rest, brethren, whatever is true, whatever is worthy of reverence and is honorable and seemly, whatever is just, whatever is pure, whatever is lovely and lovable, whatever is kind and winsome and gracious, if there is any virtue and excellence, if there is anything worthy of praise, think on and weigh and take account of these things [fix your minds on them]. - Philippians 4:6-8 (AMPC)

Pray at all times (on every occasion, in every season) in the Spirit, with all [manner of] prayer and entreaty. To that end keep alert and watch with strong purpose and perseverance, interceding in behalf of all the saints (God's consecrated people). - Ephesians 6:18 (AMPC)

Day 5

He Helps Our Relationships

One of the major complaints in life is the dissatisfaction in our relationships because of unmet expectations, disappointments, feeling neglected or rejected, and unhappiness. We all have experienced these things one time or another; be it in any relationship but more so marriages. I think we enter marriage with all these preconceived notions based on the dating and romance period of the relationship, and finally, when we must spend every waking moment with the person we were so in love with we realize we have married a different person. We come to a harsh reality that marriage takes a lot more than dating; it takes commitment and some real work. We live in a culture so sense-driven, once the emotions run low it indicates to leave and be on to the next new thing.

I think you would agree with me here that making our relationships work would require the help of the Holy Spirit. Feelings can change in a moment but to love someone with all their faults and flaws would take a greater power within us and I am so thankful for the Helper – Holy Spirit.

The Apostle Paul offers us some powerful advice, and it is all based on being filled with the Spirit. In relationships men long for respect and women long for love and affection, the man wants to know he is the head of his home and can provide for his family and a woman wants to know she is the center of her husband's world. But in reality, a man will do his duty to make sure he is a provider, and in that providing, he assumes his wife knows she is loved while the wife must be complimented, and adored. When a man works a long day, all he wants to do is come home grab the remote and unwind, and the wife wants to talk about the day and dinner plans. So how are we to maintain peace, harmony, love, and romance when we are on such opposite ends of the spectrum? Only the Holy Spirit can help us here.

The Apostle Paul urges us not to be drunk with wine but to be filled with the Spirit. (Eph 5:18). Wine releases natural brain chemicals that produce pleasurable feelings; it makes us happy, but too much wine then leads to drunkenness. Apostle Paul says wine can make you happy for a moment but continue to be filled with the Spirit which will lead to full-time joy. He advises us to sing and speak the psalms and hymns this must be an ongoing filling. We can't be filled with what we ate yesterday so to we can't be filled and led by the Spirit just once a week when we go to church. We must spend time daily being filled with the Spirit and only then can a husband love his wife the way she desires to be loved and only then can a wife respect and submit to her husband. The Holy Spirit is all the help we need in succeeding in life and I hope you would acknowledge and desire him more in your life.

Holy Spirit, come into every area of my life and help me live a life filled and led by you.

DAILY SCRIPTURES FOR MEDITATION

And I will ask the Father, and He will give you another Comforter (Counselor, Helper, Intercessor, Advocate, Strengthener, and Standby), that He may remain with you forever. - John 14:16 (AMPC)

Therefore He says, Awake, O sleeper, and arise from the dead, and Christ shall shine (make day dawn) upon you and give you light. Look carefully then how you walk! Live purposefully and worthily and accurately, not as the unwise and witless, but as wise (sensible, intelligent people), Making the very most of the time [buying up each opportunity], because the days are evil. Therefore do not be vague and thoughtless and foolish, but understanding and firmly grasping what the will of the Lord is. And do not get drunk with wine, for that is debauchery; but ever be filled and stimulated with the [Holy] Spirit. Speak out to one another in psalms and hymns and spiritual songs, offering praise with voices [and instruments] and making melody with all your heart to the Lord, At all times and for everything giving thanks in the name of our Lord Jesus Christ to God the Father. Be subject to one another out of reverence for Christ (the Messiah, the Anointed One). Wives, be subject (be submissive and adapt yourselves) to your own husbands as [a service] to the Lord. For the husband is head of the wife as Christ is the Head of the church, Himself the Savior of [His] body. As the church is subject to Christ, so let wives also be subject in everything to their husbands. Husbands, love your wives, as Christ loved the church and gave

Himself up for her. Ephesians 5:14 – 25 (AMPC)

Reflections

_____

_____

_____

_____

_____

_____

_____

_____

_____

_____

_____

_____

_____

_____

_____

_____

_____

_____

_____

_____

_____

_____

_____

_____

_____

Plan 14

THE GOOD, BAD AND UGLY

===

ALL things are working for your good! As a believer, we are constantly faced with trials in our lives. Sometimes we may think that God is being unfair to us or may have even forgotten about us, but as we review the life of Queen Esther, I trust you will have a God perspective when the storms are raging, and fires keep igniting because ALL things are working for your good.

Day 1

All Things Are Working For Your Good

How often have you heard the statement, "All things are working for your good"? I am sure within your Christian lifetime at least once or twice you have heard it. I find it so easy to use this very statement to encourage others when bad stuff happens to them, but somehow when bad things happen, it is so tough to accept it for myself. It is never easy when going through hurts and pain, disappoints and heartbreak, loss and lack, sickness and disease and obstacles and blockages to see how on earth these tragedies are working for our good. Because the world has been broken by sin and we have an enemy of our soul, bad things will always happen as long as he (Satan) is around. Jesus' work on the cross was powerful and empowers us to be over-comers of the evil one, but not everyone has accepted the way of Jesus hence giving the enemy ample room to spin his web of chaos and confusion still.

Sometimes all the bad things only happen to righteous people, and the unrighteous seems to enjoy life with no problems. I am sure you also have noticed this around you, it looks like we always have a fire to put out and there is barely any breathing room between these fires that rage in our lives. These fires may come in sickness, frustration on the job or relationships and financial issues just to list a few. No matter what our age, color of our skin, status or position we all have things happening in our lives that just does not seem to line up with what God has promised.

So how do we come to a place where we can believe the statement, "All things are working for your good"? The Bible tells us that all scripture was written to teach us so when going through tough times, we can look at the stories from the bible and find hope to go on even in our trials - (Romans 15:4 NIV). Without knowledge of the stories in the Bible, we would find ourselves at a dead end that allows the enemy to drive us to despair further. Reading the word of God and pondering on the stories will cause you to see further than your present circumstances because the word is alive and infused with the power to release hope when all seems lost.

I've heard the saying, "Hindsight is always 20/20, " and there is so much truth packed into that statement. As a child growing up in a single parent home with much neglect, later on in an alcoholic home with much abuse, a failed marriage, chasing the American dream just lost in the big city of New York and so much more, yet while facing each level of hurt and pain I could have never seen how those things could be working for my good. But as I look back I can tell you every ounce of pain, hurt, neglect, rejection, and disappointments have led me to a place of higher ground, and now with every good, bad and ugly situation that presents itself I can declare, "All things are working for my good!"

DAILY SCRIPTURES FOR MEDITATION

We are assured and know that [God being a partner in their labor] all things work together and are [fitting into a plan] for good to and for those who love God and are called according to [His] design and purpose. - Romans 8:28 (AMPC)

For whatever was thus written in former days was written for our instruction, that by [our steadfast and patient] endurance and the encouragement [drawn] from the Scriptures we might hold fast to and cherish hope. - Romans 15:4 (AMPC)

Day 2

People With A God-purpose Will Always Attract Opposition

From the inception of time, in a place of perfection in the Garden of Eden, Satan infiltrated and brought chaos. The nation of Israel has been at the end of opposition since they were called God's chosen people. People who have chosen the path of God will always be met with the fiercest of opposition. In my earlier years as a young Christian I use to believe that all the trouble in my life was because of my disobedience even though I worked hard to please God, but as I matured in Christ I recognize that all the trouble that comes my way is not because of me doing something wrong, but it is because I'm walking in my purpose. So I want to encourage you today; don't view the trouble in your life as punishment from God but know that if you have purposed in your heart to go after the God-life, you are a moving target for the enemy which you already have the victory over.

I want to touch on the life of Esther over the next few days hoping you will draw strength, hope, and courage to keep going even though you are in a rough place right now. Esther was a Jewish orphan girl adopted by her cousin Mordecai. They lived in the city of Susa ruled by a powerful king named Xerxes. This king held a huge banquet for many royal dignitaries and wanted to show off the beauty of his wife to them all. When he called for Queen Vashti, she refused to show up embarrassing the king at the highest level imagined. Because of this disrespect the king sought council and stopped Queen Vashti from ever appearing before him again, and she was to be replaced by someone better. This was in hopes all women throughout the land will know this behavior will not be tolerated by the kings and nobles of the land.

A search ensued for the most beautiful, young virgins in all the land to be brought to the palace for a year of beauty preparations before they could be presented to the king; it sure sounds like the miss universe pageant. To a beautiful young woman who had no parents, living in a land where her ethnic background was not considered as much this must sound like a dream come true. Being able to live in the king's palace, eating the best foods, drinking the best wine, soaking in exquisite perfumes, oils and cosmetics...Oh yes, heaven come! This search could not have come at a better time, at least for the next twelve months Esther would experience the life of royalty, acceptance, status, and hope for a bright future. Esther gets chosen and immediately finds favor with Hegai the one in charge of the harem, and he gives her preferential treatment. Here again, we get a glimpse of perfection, peace and a chance for a good life for Esther.

I am sure like Esther there have been opportunities where everything seems to look up, dreams are finally coming through, and finally, you breathe a sigh of relief because you see the light at the end of the tunnel; only to discover trouble would soon crouch at the door. Esther and her people would soon be nearly at extinction. How could this be working for her good? Don't lose hope we will explore more as the days go by!

DAILY SCRIPTURES FOR MEDITATION

We are assured and know that [God being a partner in their labor] all things work together and are [fitting into a plan] for good to and for those who love God and are called according to [His] design and purpose. - Romans 8:28 (AMPC)

On the seventh day, when King Xerxes was in high spirits from wine,he commanded the seven eunuchs who served him— Mehuman, Biztha, Harbona, Bigtha, Abagtha, Zethar and Karkas— to bring before him Queen Vashti, wearing her royal crown, in order to display her beauty to the people and nobles, for she was lovely to look at. But when the attendants delivered the king's command, Queen Vashti refused to come. Then the king became furious and burned with anger.
"According to law, what must be done to Queen Vashti?" he asked. "She has not obeyed the command of King Xerxes that the eunuchs have taken to her." - Esther 1:10-12,15 (NIV)

Now there was in the citadel of Susa a Jew of the tribe of Benjamin, named Mordecai, son of Jair, the son of Shimei, the son of Kish, who had been carried into exile from Jerusalem by Nebuchadnezzar king of Babylon, among those taken captive with Jehoiachin[a] king of

Judah. Mordecai had a cousin named Hadassah, whom he had brought up because she had neither father nor mother. This young woman, who was also known as Esther, had a lovely figure and was beautiful. Mordecai had taken her as his own daughter when her father and mother died.

When the king's order and edict had been proclaimed, many young women were brought to the citadel of Susa and put under the care of Hegai. Esther also was taken to the king's palace and entrusted to Hegai, who had charge of the harem. She pleased him and won his favor. Immediately he provided her with her beauty treatments and special food. He assigned to her seven female attendants selected from the king's palace and moved her and her attendants into the best place in the harem. - Esther 2:5-9 (NIV)

Day 3

Fulfilling Your God-purpose Is Bigger Than You

I am sure you are excited to read on as it is so refreshing to know that great people in the Bible faced situations like us and overcame and now gives us a shot of adrenaline to keep going. Now that Esther is in the palace, enjoying a life she could only dream about her cousin sends word to her that things are about to become topsy-turvy.

Esther won the heart of the king among all her competition, and he crowned her as Queen to replace Vashti, and a banquet was held in her honor. Through all this time Esther had a secret she was a Jew. No way would she have been allowed a chance with the King had her nationality been known.

Mordecai got hold of a conspiracy while Esther was queen, a plot was made to kill the king and Mordecai sent word to Esther who then told the king giving credit to Mordecai for the information. When an investigation was done, it proved to be true, and the guilty were put to death. No credit was given to Mordecai, but at least the king's life was spared. In the process of time the king honored a man named Haman, he was given a seat higher than any other nobles in the palace. He received honor from all the king's officials at the king's gate where Mordecai also served, but Mordecai refused to bow down to him.

Mordecai was a Jew that took God's laws at heart and bowing down to a man would be breaking the rule of all rules, "Thou shall have no other god's before me" That was a big no, no! In like manner when you serve God with all your heart, when you decide to not follow the crowd or blend in with the culture around you, most definitely you will find yourself persecuted. Mordecai's behavior angered Haman so much he didn't just want Mordecai's life but all his people.

Understand that the enemy is not only after you but the generations that will come out of you and after you. If the righteous may live, then it is only natural they will produce offspring that will hopefully be righteous. To deter the production of righteous offspring the enemy tries to stop righteousness in its tracks by wiping out an entire generation at a time. We always must remember the enemy seeks only to, "Steal, kill and destroy" (John 10:10).

Haman plotted the demise of all the Jews within the kingdom of King Xerxes, and he waited for the opportune time to petition the king for the approval to do so. Haman convinced the king there was living among them a group of people that separate themselves from all the other people of the land and their customs were different hence they disobeyed the king's laws.

The Apostle Paul also warns us today to be separated and different from the rest of the world and as a result it will always make us a target. I want you to see those who pursue God's purpose will always face hard times, troubles and trials. The king gave Haman the permission he needed to now go after the people of God. A decree was written out and distributed to all kings throughout the land to kill all Jews on one specific day which was the thirteenth day of the twelfth month; the month called Adar. The Jews would now have to be annihilated, and all they possessed would be taken from them. How can this be working for Esther and her people as good?

DAILY SCRIPTURES FOR MEDITATION

We are assured and know that [God being a partner in their labor] all things work together and are [fitting into a plan] for good to and for those who love God and are called according to [His] design and purpose. - Romans 8:28 (AMPC)

The thief comes only to steal and kill and destroy; I have come that they may have life, and have it to the full. - John 10:10 (NIV)

Do not conform to the pattern of this world, but be transformed by the renewing of your mind. Then you will be able to test and approve what God's will is—his good, pleasing and perfect will. - Romans 12:2 (NIV)

Then Haman said to King Xerxes, "There is a certain people dispersed among the peoples in all the provinces of your kingdom who keep themselves separate. Their customs are different from those of all other people, and they do not obey the king's laws; it is not in the king's best interest to tolerate them. If it pleases the king, let a decree be issued to destroy them, and I will give ten thousand talents[b] of silver to the king's administrators for the royal treasury." So the king took his signet ring from his finger and gave it to Haman, son of Hammedatha, the Agagite, the enemy of the Jews. "Keep the money," the king said to Haman, "and do with the people as you please." - Esther 3:8-10 (NIV)

Day 4

While Fulfilling The God-purpose, It Will Always Seem The Enemy Is Winning

The Jews are scheduled to be wiped out! How often you are going through a situation in your life, and you are convinced this will be the end of you, or you have no more strength to go on, you don't even have a prayer in you. The enemy has finally won, and you just don't have the faith to believe anymore, you feel alone, and this could the end! Well, Mordecai felt this same way once the news hit the kingdom. There was a great sense of defeat, loss, and mourning throughout the land. Esther got word from Mordecai what was about to happen and enlisted her help, and at first, she thought to herself, "I can do nothing!" Because the law stated that if anyone approached the king without being called and he was not for seeing them, they would be killed. Initially, Esther took a position she could do nothing to help because her life would be on the line. It didn't take her long to realize from Mordecai that her life was on the line anyway because the fact is she was also a Jew.

Esther looked at her present circumstances and decided she couldn't help because she would be killed but when Mordecai put perspective in her way she changed her mind about what could be done. Sometimes in our own lives, our present state and circumstances can cause us to be blinded to the promises of God's word, and we can live in defeat thinking there is nothing more I can do. Maybe there isn't anything you can do in your situation but calling out to God is always the thing we must do. Mordecai showed Esther her purpose, and it was not just to enjoy the palace and the benefits that came with it but to see beyond it, he wanted her to see the purpose of the position and the pain. Sometimes we must surround ourselves with people who will pull us up, set us straight and remind us we were created on purpose for purpose.

Esther then calls for a kingdom-wide fast and prayer for three days among all the fellow Jews. She settled in her heart if she would die it would be for a noble cause of at least trying to save her people and generations to come. You may not feel like you want to go forward right now because the enemy may have pulled out all the stops, maybe the sickness in your body is getting worse rather than better, maybe you just got laid off from your job, and you have no savings, maybe you are nearly at divorce and have no hope, maybe your business seems to go under and it just feels like the enemy is gaining ground. Today, I want to encourage you just like Esther when there was nothing else to do physically, call your church friends, your husband, your wife, your intercessors and do a fast for a few days and just pray to Abba (Father) for wisdom, strength, and favor to make it through this time. Esther's fast and prayer were done to find favor with the king so she could plead her case for her people and expose the plans of the enemy.

You already have an audience with the King because of what Jesus did for you so don't let the situation in your life, even though it is bad, keep you from fulfilling your God-purpose. Seek him, plead your case and see him make a way.

DAILY SCRIPTURES FOR MEDITATION

We are assured and know that [God being a partner in their labor] all things work together and are [fitting into a plan] for good to and for those who love God and are called according to [His] design and purpose. - Romans 8:28 (AMPC)

So Hathak went out to Mordecai in the open square of the city in front of the king's gate. Mordecai told him everything that had happened to him, including the exact amount of money Haman had promised to pay into the royal treasury for the destruction of the Jews. He also gave him a copy of the text of the edict for their annihilation, which had been published in Susa, to show to Esther and explain it to her, and he told him to instruct her to go into the king's presence to beg for mercy and plead with him for her people. Hathak went back and reported to Esther what Mordecai had said. Then she instructed him to say to Mordecai, "All the king's officials and the people of the royal provinces know that for any man or woman who approaches the king in the inner court without being summoned the king has but one law: that they be put to death unless the king extends the gold scepter to them and spares their lives. But thirty days have passed since I was called to go to the king." - Esther 4:6-11 (NIV)

When Esther's words were reported to Mordecai, he sent back this answer: "Do not think that because you are in the king's house, you alone of all the Jews will escape. For if you remain silent at this time, relief and deliverance for the Jews will arise from another place, but you and your father's family will perish. And who knows but that you have come to your royal position for such a time as this?"

Then Esther sent this reply to Mordecai: "Go, gather together all the Jews who are in Susa, and fast for me. Do not eat or drink for three days, night or day. I and my attendants will fast as you do. When this is done, I will go to the king, even though it is against the law. And if I perish, I perish." So Mordecai went away and carried out all of Esther's instructions. - Esther 4:12-17 (NIV)

Day 5

What The Enemy Means For Evil The Lord Will Use For Your Good

After the fast, Esther gained wisdom from God on how to approach the king, make her request and expose the enemy. God was truly with her, and he was working behind the scenes to bring good out of what was meant for evil. Queen Esther invited the king and Haman to a private banquet, the king was so excited to be with her and would give her anything she asked for. Haman was ecstatic that he was the only one invited with the king to be with Queen Esther. She didn't make her request right away and invited them to come the next day to dine again with her. Haman left the queen feeling elated, but when he saw Mordecai, his rage burned within him. Every time the enemy sees the child of God living out their purpose it causes the enemy to be angry. Haman goes away and plots with his friends and wife how to kill Mordecai. So he build a huge gallows to have Mordecai hanged.

Always remember when we pray and seek God's help he will never leave us stranded, all the while you are going through hardships and trials if you set your heart to seek God in it he will make a way. That night after meeting with Esther the king could not sleep and he sent for his book of chronicles to be read to him. Lo and behold he comes across the record of the plot to take his life, and Mordecai's name was recorded, and he enquired what honor was done for him. His servants replied, "Nothing was done." How often do you feel like God just does not see or remember our good deeds? I want you to know nothing escapes his eyes and we will reap if we do not give up. Haman was in the courts, and the king called for him and asked his opinion on what honor should be given to a person who saved his life? Right away Haman assumed it was himself the king was talking about, and he pulled out all the stops for honoring the person.

Haman suggested a royal robe the king has worn be put on the person, a horse the king had ridden, and the person should be led through the entire city pronouncing, "This is what is done for the man the king delights to honor!" This excited the king, and he sent Haman to prepare the stuff to have this done at once for Mordecai and

Haman had to do it. Oh, how he was grieved! Don't forget all things are working for your good once you set your heart and mind on him who is able. Haman was enraged and had to go to the banquet with Queen Esther, and this time she would make her request and expose the enemy. The king was outraged and left the room when he discovered Haman was the enemy. Haman tried to beg the queen to save him but he launched at her, and the king saw him, his anger burned that Haman had no respect for his queen. Haman was taken away immediately and was hanged on the same pole he set up for Mordecai.

This story gives me so much strength to go on in difficult and impossible times, Esther and Mordecai lives were plagued with good, bad and ugly times but supported by each other and the seeking of their God they overcame the evil one. Esther inherited the estate of Haman, and the king took back his ring he had given to Haman and gave it to Mordecai and Esther gave Haman's estate to Mordecai to run. The law was overturned to destroy the Jews, and a new law gave them the right to protect themselves from any present and future danger. They gained the victory through every bad and ugly situation. I hope you would read the book of Esther on your own time and revisit this book in times of struggle because it is infused with hope for a people who lean on the arm of God. God is greater than any evil; we must believe.

DAILY SCRIPTURES FOR MEDITATION

We are assured and know that [God being a partner in their labor] all things work together and are [fitting into a plan] for good to and for those who love God and are called according to [His] design and purpose. - Romans 8:28 (AMPC)

On the third day, Esther put on her royal robes and stood in the inner court of the palace, in front of the king's hall. The king was sitting on his royal throne in the hall, facing the entrance. When he saw Queen Esther standing in the court, he was pleased with her and held out to her the gold scepter that was in his hand. So Esther approached and touched the tip of the scepter.

Then the king asked, "What is it, Queen Esther? What is your request?

Even up to half the kingdom, it will be given you."

"If it pleases the king," replied Esther, "let the king, together with Haman, come today to a banquet I have prepared for him."

"Bring Haman at once," the king said, "so that we may do what Esther asks."

So the king and Haman went to the banquet Esther had prepared. As they were drinking wine, the king again asked Esther, "Now what is your petition? It will be given you. And what is your request? Even up to half the kingdom, it will be granted." - Esther 5:1-6 (NIV)

"What honor and recognition has Mordecai received for this?" the king asked.

"Nothing has been done for him," his attendants answered.

The king said, "Who is in the court?" Now Haman had just entered the outer court of the palace to speak to the king about impaling Mordecai on the pole he had set up for him.

His attendants answered, "Haman is standing in the court."

"Bring him in," the king ordered.

When Haman entered, the king asked him, "What should be done for the man the king delights to honor?"

Now Haman thought to himself, "Who is there that the king would rather honor than me?" So he answered the king, "For the man, the king delights to honor, have them bring a royal robe the king has worn and a horse the king has ridden, one with a royal crest placed on its head. Then let the robe and horse be entrusted to one of the king's most noble princes. Let them robe the man the king delights to honor, and lead him on the horse through the city streets, proclaiming before him, 'This is what is done for the man the king delights to honor!'"

"Go at once," the king commanded Haman. "Get the robe and the horse and do just as you have suggested for Mordecai the Jew, who sits at the king's gate. Do not neglect anything you have recommended."

So Haman got the robe and the horse. He robed Mordecai, and led him on horseback through the city streets, proclaiming before him, "This is what is done for the man the king delights to honor!" - Esther 6:3-11 (NIV)

So the king and Haman went to Queen Esther's banquet, and as they were drinking wine on the second day, the king again asked, "Queen

Esther, what is your petition? It will be given you. What is your request? Even up to half the kingdom, it will be granted."

Then Queen Esther answered, "If I have found favor with you, Your Majesty, and if it pleases you, grant me my life—this is my petition. And spare my people—this is my request. For I and my people have been sold to be destroyed, killed and annihilated. If we had merely been sold as male and female slaves, I would have kept quiet, because no such distress would justify disturbing the king."

King Xerxes asked Queen Esther, "Who is he? Where is he—the man who has dared to do such a thing?"

Esther said, "An adversary and enemy! This vile Haman!"

Then Haman was terrified before the king and queen. The king got up in a rage, left his wine and went out into the palace garden. But Haman, realizing that the king had already decided his fate, stayed behind to beg Queen Esther for his life.

Just as the king returned from the palace garden to the banquet hall, Haman was falling on the couch where Esther was reclining.

The king exclaimed, "Will he even molest the queen while she is with me in the house?"

As soon as the word left the king's mouth, they covered Haman's face. Then Harbona, one of the eunuchs attending the king, said, "A pole reaching to a height of fifty cubits[b] stands by Haman's house. He had it set up for Mordecai, who spoke up to help the king."

The king said, "Impale him on it!" So they impaled Haman on the pole he had set up for Mordecai. Then the king's fury subsided. - Esther 7:1-10 (NIV)

Reflections

Plan 15

THE POWER OF PRAYER

==

Prayer to most believers is viewed as monotonous. But the truth is prayer is powerful, and it is a time set apart where we converse with our heavenly Father. The privilege of prayer is far greater than petitioning for our needs, but rather it is the positioning posture for miracles to invade our sphere of influence. After you have finished with this plan, my prayer for you is that you would never view prayer the same as before.

Day 1

Prayer Is The Practice Of The Presence Of God

Prayer is the Practice of the Presence of God. It is the place where pride is abandoned, hope is lifted, and supplication is made. Prayer is the place of admitting our need, of adopting humility and claiming dependence upon God. Prayer is the needful practice of the Christian. Prayer is the exercise of faith and hope. Prayer is the privilege of touching the heart of the Father through the Son of God, Jesus our Lord- Matt Slick.

Prayer is an inexhaustible topic, and no matter how often we hear sermons or read books on prayer, we can always glean something new on this subject. When one takes the posture of prayer it is a sign of great humility because it is in this act we recognize there is someone greater than us, and we need his help. Prayer is so much more than just asking God to do stuff for us, to bless us, to open doors for us, and nothing is wrong with asking God we are encouraged by Jesus to ask and keep on asking. (Matthew 7:7)

But prayer is the actual practice of the presence of God, this statement gives prayer so much more meaning because so often we pray on the go, or we are rushing to catch the seven o' clock headlines on the news, or we had a long day, and we just want to get to bed early. No matter what the reason, we all have experienced rushing prayer. Practicing the presence of God means I must take time to sit, pushing aside everything else, ready to engage in conversation giving God my full attention.

Sometimes I find it easier to understand spiritual things by comparing them to the natural. So if we are talking about practicing someone's presence, we can look at the relationship between a husband and wife. Often I am in the same room with my husband, lying on the same bed, and he is catching up on emails, and I am reading; we are in each other's presence, but we are not practicing each other's presence. But if we put everything aside and we engage in conversation, we then practice each other's presence. So too with prayer, we can talk to God but all the while our minds and hearts are no way connected to him. I know this feeling in my times of on-purpose prayer my mind becomes the most bombarded with my to-do list. I have learned over the years not to view prayer as a chore or work, but as the act of practicing God's presence, therefore prayer has become more of a delight for me.

If you struggle with prayer or are intimidated because you don't have all the right words, or you run out of things to pray about I want to encourage you to start off slowly by coming into a quiet place with some soft worship music, this will help you sense God's presence and then you can share your heart in your own words, and that will lead you to great times of prayer.

"Prayer is not learned in a classroom but in the closet." E. M. Bounds

DAILY SCRIPTURES FOR MEDITATION

"Here's what I want you to do: Find a quiet, secluded place so you won't be tempted to role-play before God. Just be there as simply and honestly as you can manage. The focus will shift from you to God, and you will begin to sense his grace." - Matthew 6:6 (MSG)

Day 2

Prayer Brings God's Desires From Heaven To Earth

"Our prayers lay the track down which God's power can come. Like a mighty locomotive, his power is irresistible, but it cannot reach us without rails." Watchman Nee

As we spend time in God's presence, we catch his heart. Can you remember the time you dated? Do you remember the feelings of awe and wonder, the anticipation of spending time with the person and the sorrow to leave; time just was not enough. But one of the most important things about spending time with the person you love is the attention you pay to them while they share what's in their heart with you. The disciples spent a lot of time with Jesus and the time caused them to want to know more. They had seen him do many miracles and wonders, they had seen him spend countless hours in prayer, and so they wanted to tap into his heart, and they asked Jesus to teach them to pray –

"Do not be like them, for your Father knows what you need before you ask him. "This, then, is how you should pray: "'Our Father in heaven, hallowed be your name, your kingdom come, your will be done, on earth as it is in heaven." Matthew 6:8-10 (NIV)

Jesus then ventured out to give them the model of prayer that would revolutionize not only their lives but ours also; it is a prayer we are still praying over two thousand years later – Heaven Come! I find it interesting that Jesus did not teach the disciples to pray for themselves or their needs first, but the priority of the prayer was that God's name would forever be kept Holy and then for God's domain to reach ours – "This, then, is how you should pray: "'Our Father in heaven, hallowed be your name," (Matthew 6:9 NIV). How powerful is that? So often we approach prayer for our needs only, but true prayer pushes past our agendas to get to the heart of the King. I know there are all types of prayers and at different times in our lives we may have different needs, and that may drive the direction of our prayers, but as a believer growing and maturing in the Lord, our prayers now should always be shaped by the priority of what is on

God's heart.

You may ask the question, "Well if I don't pray for my needs how will they be met?" But just before Jesus introduced the model prayer to his disciples, he reminded them their heavenly Father knows what they have need of even before they ask Him. "Do not be like them, for your Father knows what you need before you ask him." (Matthew 6:8-10 NIV). God wants us to know that he cares about our needs like an earthly parent cares for their children, so our requirements need not be the priority on our prayer list. But desiring God's name and kingdom to reach earth is by far the most excellent prayer we could ever pray. If you have never prayed this way before, today I want to encourage you to take just a few minutes and ask God to share his heart with you so you can bring heaven to earth.

"We must begin to believe that God, in the mystery of prayer, has entrusted us with a force that can move the Heavenly world, and can bring its power down to earth." Andrew Murray

DAILY SCRIPTURES FOR MEDITATION

"Here's what I want you to do: Find a quiet, secluded place so you won't be tempted to role-play before God. Just be there as simply and honestly as you can manage. The focus will shift from you to God, and you will begin to sense his grace." - Matthew 6:6 (MSG)

Day 3

Prayer Is Our Winning Weapon In The Invisible War

"Church fails to pray, God's cause decays, and evil of every kind prevails. In other words, God works through the prayers of His people, and when they fail Him at this point, decline and deadness ensue." - E.M Bounds

We all know there are wars and rumors of wars raging wild across the earth because the news and social media give it more than enough coverage, yet when a spiritual battle comes up we have a hard time believing this is real. But Jesus reminds us to be mindful of the war raging. He said, "Watch and pray so that you will not fall into temptation. The spirit is willing, but the flesh is weak." (Matthew 26:41 AMP). From this statement, we can recognize that the war is mostly internal for the believer. Jesus made this statement the night he was about to be taken away to be crucified; he had just completed the Passover meal with his disciples, and he took a few disciples to the garden for support in prayer because he knew what was about to befall him. After a while of praying Jesus came back and saw the disciples sleeping, and he said, "Then he returned to his disciples and found them sleeping. "Couldn't you men keep watch with me for one hour?" he asked Peter." (Matthew 26:40).

Jesus was emphasizing the importance of prayer in this on-going battle is to keep the faith. The faith to believe he is who he says he is and he will do what he says he will do, is the biggest struggle we all face. When money is running low, when our children are going off the righteous path after we have done everything to teach them God's ways, when sickness and pain are wreaking havoc in our bodies and worries seem to be the bed we lie in every night, when our relationships are plagued with disloyalty and cheating, when the business or ministry have taken the best years of our lives, and it still seems to go under, when there is alcohol and abuse in our homes trust me it takes a real fight to still believe God and his word. But thank God for prayer because it is the one comfort we have knowing that through it all, through the raging winds and storms of life and through the struggle and hardships we can get with other saints and send up a prayer to God and know that he hears and he will answer.

Jesus shared with the Apostle Peter the plan the enemy had for his life, Jesus didn't hold back in letting him know the enemy was after him but he also gave Peter the solution to the problem. "Simon, Simon (Peter), listen! Satan has demanded permission to sift [all of] you like grain; but I have prayed [especially] for you [Peter], that your faith [and confidence in Me] may not fail; and you, once you have turned back again [to Me], strengthen and support your brothers [in the faith]." (Luke 22:31-32 AMP). The plan of the enemy has been the same through the ages to get us to doubt God, and his word and the strategy remains the same still today; watch and pray!

"If you are strangers to prayer you are strangers to power" –
Billy Sunday.

DAILY SCRIPTURES FOR MEDITATION

Finally, be strong in the Lord and in his mighty power. Put on the full armor of God, so that you can take your stand against the devil's schemes. For our struggle is not against flesh and blood, but against the rulers, against the authorities, against the powers of this dark world and against the spiritual forces of evil in the heavenly realms. - Ephesians 6:10-12 (NIV)

God's Word is an indispensable weapon. In the same way, prayer is essential in this ongoing warfare. Pray hard and long. Pray for your brothers and sisters. Keep your eyes open. Keep each other's spirits up so that no one falls behind or drops out. - Ephesians 6:18 (MSG)

Day 4

Don't Quit Praying

"Perseverance in prayer is not overcoming God's reluctance but rather laying hold of God's willingness. Our sovereign God has purposed to sometimes require persevering prayer as the means to accomplish His will." – William Thrasher

Have you ever felt like you have been praying and the answers are not forthcoming? It seems like the heavens are shut up, and the Lord has fallen asleep on you, and no matter how hard you try to stay in faith, the fear of the answer not coming takes ahold of your heart and mind. Well, you are not alone, there are times in our lives when we all feel like we are in the desert, but there are answers to press in for even if it takes a while.

The prophet Daniel in the bible is a great example on persevering prayer, and he had a disciplined prayer life; three times a day Daniel would bow and pray whether things were good or bad in his life. (Daniel 6:10)

Daniel didn't have life easy, he was taken away into captivity, forced to live under a new name and religious ways, and he was thrown into a lion's den because he would not conform to the culture of his day, yet, he never moved away from the discipline of prayer. Because of his obedience to God, he was entrusted with visions of the future, though the visions were dreadful he purposed to seek God for understanding through prayer and fasting. Daniel persevered for three weeks in constant searching for understanding. Sometimes we buy into a lie that if we continue to pray for an answer for a long period we are repetitious and we stop short. I've come to understand there are just some things we must keep on praying for, e.g., unsaved loved ones, healing in bodies and marriages, laws and legislation that represents the kingdom of God, and this is just a few.

Daniel had an encounter with an angel at the end of his fast, and the angel said to him, "Do not be afraid, Daniel. Since the first day that you set your mind to gain understanding and to humble yourself before your God, your words were heard, and I have come in response to them." (Daniel 10:12 NIV).

Isn't that amazing? After three weeks of prayer, the answer finally came, but I want you to pay close attention to the verse above, "Since the first day." From the first day, Daniel set out to pray the angel was sent with the answer but was held up by an evil force that kept the answer from coming. Daniel persevered in prayer, and it strengthened the angel to fight and eventually break through with the answer. I want to encourage you today; please don't quit praying because your answer might be on the way!

On persevering prayer: "I look at a stone cutter hammering away at a rock a hundred times without so much as a crack showing in it. Yet at the 101ˢᵗ blow, it splits in two. I know it was not the one blow that did it, but all that had gone before."
Jacob August Riis

DAILY SCRIPTURES FOR MEDITATION

So these administrators and satraps went as a group to the king and said: "May King Darius live forever! The royal administrators, prefects, satraps, advisers, and governors have all agreed that the king should issue an edict and enforce the decree that anyone who prays to any god or human being during the next thirty days, except to you, Your Majesty, shall be thrown into the lions' den. Now, Your Majesty, issue the decree and put it in writing so that it cannot be altered—in accordance with the law of the Medes and Persians, which cannot be repealed." So King Darius put the decree in writing.
Now when Daniel learned that the decree had been published, he went home to his upstairs room where the windows opened toward Jerusalem. Three times a day he got down on his knees and prayed, giving thanks to his God, just as he had done before. - Daniel 6:6-9 (NIV)

I, Daniel, was the only one who saw the vision; those who were with me did not see it, but such terror overwhelmed them that they fled and hid themselves. So I was left alone, gazing at this great vision; I had no strength left, my face turned deathly pale, and I was helpless. Then I heard him speaking, and as I listened to him, I fell into a deep sleep, my face to the ground. - Daniel 10:7-9 (NIV)

Then he continued, "Do not be afraid, Daniel. Since the first day that you set your mind to gain understanding and to humble yourself before your God, your words were heard, and I have come in response to them. But the prince of the Persian kingdom resisted me twenty-one days. Then Michael, one of the chief princes, came to help me, because I was detained there with the king of Persia. Now I have come to explain to you what will happen to your people in the future, for the vision concerns a time yet to come." - Daniel 10:12-14 (NIV)

Day 5

Prayer Opens The Door For Miracles

"When human reason has exhausted every possibility, the children can go to their Father and receive all they need. ... For only when you have become utterly dependent upon prayer and faith, only when all human possibilities have been exhausted, can you begin to reckon that God will intervene and work His miracles." – Basilea Schlink

I am so thankful for the simplicity of prayer that wrought great victories in impossible situations in our lives. Jesus, when teaching his disciples to pray was actually equipping them to access the courtroom of heaven, shatter spiritual glass ceilings, and enlist the help of the greatest angelic army to bring heaven to earth. The privilege of prayer is far greater than petitioning for our needs, but rather it is the positioning posture for miracles to invade our sphere of influence. Jesus never took prayer lightly, and he being the Son of God had set times of prayer daily, early mornings, and sometimes all night. His secluded times of prayer was his refueling port and gaining the heart of his father; what was on God's agenda for the day. If Jesus did not skip prayer how much more important it is for us to have set times of prayer also.

Many miracles were done through Jesus because he was committed to prayer. He healed everyone that came to him for healing, he raised the dead, he fed thousands of people with limited food, he walked on water, and he endured the crucifixion and death, and every miracle was preceded by prayer. Jesus said, Greater things we will do. (John 14:12) The Apostles walked in the measure of prayer just like Jesus did and they also saw great miracles in their lives. The Apostle Peter was imprisoned overnight, heavily guarded awaiting his trial the next day and the bible says, "So Peter was kept in prison, but the church was earnestly praying to God for him." (Acts 12:5 NIV). Because of the prayers of the saints, an angel was enabled to intervene and break Peter out of the prison cell.

When we pray on earth the will and heart of God, it may seem like nothing is happening but according to the book of Revelation, our prayers are going up to heaven and is stored in golden bowls.

(Revelation 5:8). King David had the revelation of prayer rising like incense before the Lord. (Psalm 141:2 NIV) Later on, in Revelation, we read about the angel mingling the incense and the prayers of the saints on the altar of fire, and the smoke went up before God. These scriptures show us that our prayers are not in vain or wasted, but they go up before God and Jesus who is our perfect intercessor, prays perfect prayers for us. I am praying as you are coming to the end of this plan that your whole view and mindset of prayer have changed, and every time you approach God's throne, you would remember that your prayer is being heard and the answer will arrive in due time.

Recap:

- Prayer is the practice of the presence of God

- Prayer brings God's desires from heaven to earth

- Prayer is our winning weapon in the invisible war

- Don't quit praying

- Prayer opens the door for miracles

"God shapes the world by prayer. The more prayer there is in the world, the better the world will be, the mightier the forces against evil...." E.M. Bounds

DAILY SCRIPTURES FOR MEDITATION

But Jesus often withdrew to lonely places and prayed. - Luke 5:16 (NIV)

One of those days Jesus went out to a mountainside to pray and spent the night praying to God. - Luke 6:12 (NIV)

So Peter was kept in prison, but the church was earnestly praying to God for him.
The night before Herod was to bring him to trial, Peter was sleeping between two soldiers, bound with two chains, and sentries stood guard at the entrance. Suddenly an angel of the Lord appeared, and a light shone in the cell. He struck Peter on the side and woke him up.

"Quick, get up!" he said, and the chains fell off Peter's wrists.

Then the angel said to him, "Put on your clothes and sandals." And Peter did so. "Wrap your cloak around you and follow me," the angel told him. Peter followed him out of prison, but he had no idea that what the angel was doing was really happening; he thought he was seeing a vision. They passed the first and second guards and came to the iron gate leading to the city. It opened for them by itself, and they went through it. When they had walked the length of one street, suddenly the angel left him.

Then Peter came to himself and said, "Now I know without a doubt that the Lord has sent his angel and rescued me from Herod's clutches and from everything the Jewish people were hoping would happen."
- Acts 12:5-11(NIV)

Then I saw a Lamb, looking as if it had been slain, standing at the center of the throne, encircled by the four living creatures and the elders. The Lamb had seven horns, and seven eyes, which are the seven spirits of God sent out into all the earth. He went and took the scroll from the right hand of him who sat on the throne. And when he had taken it, the four living creatures and the twenty-four elders fell down before the Lamb. Each one had a harp, and they were holding golden bowls full of incense, which are the prayers of God's people. - Revelation 5:6-8 (NIV)

Another angel, who had a golden censer, came and stood at the altar. He was given much incense to offer, with the prayers of all God's people, on the golden altar in front of the throne. The smoke of the incense, together with the prayers of God's people, went up before God from the angel's hand. Then the angel took the censer, filled it with fire from the altar, and hurled it on the earth; and there came peals of thunder, rumblings, flashes of lightning and an earthquake. - Revelation 8:3-5 (NIV)

Reflections

_____
_____
_____
_____
_____
_____
_____
_____
_____
_____
_____
_____
_____
_____
_____
_____
_____
_____
_____
_____
_____
_____
_____
_____
_____

Plan 16

THE POWER OF
THE CROSS

==

The cross is much more than a piece of jewelry or a symbol on a building. The power behind the cross is limitless and boundless, and as believers, once we get hold of this revelation it would change our misconceptions about the cross and alter our lives forever.

Day 1

The Power Of The Cross

I have gained such an appreciation of the cross of Jesus Christ in recent years. For a long time, I struggled to understand how something so gruesome could hold so much value for my life. As my relationship with God grew, I got a better understanding of the preciousness of the cross. Many people today look at the cross as the symbol of Christianity, so they assume that if someone is wearing a cross as jewelry or has the cross tattooed that the person belongs to the Christian faith! We see crosses as the backdrop of many church stages or on the outside of church buildings elevated for all to see. The cross identifies the Christians.

The staggering truth about the cross is that while many wear it as a symbol of identity the power resident in the finished work of the cross is not known and therefore not manifested in the lives of the very ones who display it publicly. I hope that after you complete this plan, the cross will become more valuable to you than money, possessions or precious stones. I love the cross, and though today it is only recognized as a symbol the cross has become a permanent place in my long-term memory I visit every day. I find grace, peace, and joy at the very place meant to be death, shame, and scorn. The Apostle Paul makes mention to the church of Corinth that the cross seems absurd to those who are wise in their own eyes but for those who understand the cross, it is the very power of God. (1 Corinthians 1:18)

As we read about the crucifixion in John chapter 19, we are presented with a scene that incorporates all people groups like no other in history. Let us examine the scene a little closer:

1. **The Place of the crucifixion** – Golgotha translated as the place of the skull.

2. **The Symbol** – The Cross on which the innocent will die a death for the guilty.

3. **Two Thieves** – Also on crosses hanging on the right and left of Jesus; they deserved death.

4. The Judge – Pilate, holding the authority to put to death the guilty and uphold the laws of the land.

5. The Chief Priests of the Jews – The spiritual leaders' in charge of teaching the people to be spiritually fit.

6. The Roman Soldiers – The officers used to enforce and administer punishment.

7. Jesus' mother and disciples – Close family, friends and loved one.

The scene at the foot of the cross involved so many positions, titles, accolades, shame, disgrace, and diversity yet the common denominator to them all was the symbol of the cross.

Desire: Lord, help me to see the power of the cross in my life.

DAILY SCRIPTURES FOR MEDITATION

For the message of the cross is foolishness to those who are perishing, but to us who are being saved, it is the power of God. - 1 Corinthians 1:18- (NIV)

Carrying his own cross, he went out to the place of the Skull (which in Aramaic is called Golgotha). There they crucified him and with him two others—one on each side and Jesus in the middle. - John 19:17-18 (NIV)

Pilate had a notice prepared and fastened to the cross. It read: Jesus of Nazareth, the king of the Jews. Many of the Jews read this sign, for the place where Jesus was crucified was near the city, and the sign was written in Aramaic, Latin, and Greek. 21 The chief priests of the Jews protested to Pilate, "Do not write 'The King of the Jews,' but that this man claimed to be king of the Jews." Pilate answered, "What I have written, I have written." - John 19:19 – 22 (NIV)

When the soldiers crucified Jesus, they took his clothes, dividing them into four shares, one for each of them, with the undergarment remaining. This garment was seamless, woven in one piece from top to bottom. - John 19:23 – 24 (NIV)

"Let's not tear it," they said to one another. "Let's decide by lot who will get it." This happened that the scripture might be fulfilled that said, "They divided my clothes among them and cast lots for my garment." So this is what the soldiers did. - John 19:23 – 24 (NIV)

Near the cross of Jesus stood his mother, his mother's sister, Mary the wife of Clopas, and Mary Magdalene. When Jesus saw his mother there, and the disciple whom he loved standing nearby, he said to her, "Woman, here is your son," and to the disciple, "Here is your mother." From that time on, this disciple took her into his home. - John 19:25 – 27(NIV)

Day 2

At The Cross We Find Forgiveness

At the foot of the cross Jesus hung beaten beyond recognition, using every bit of energy and strength to draw his breath we get a glimpse into the depth of his breaking yet boundless heart. As he looks down from the cross he can see many people groups before him, he can hear the statements of mockery and hatred being slurred at him, he can hear the tones of anger, and he can see the soldiers laughing in scorn at yet another valueless Jew.

I can only imagine the pain Jesus must have experienced seeing and hearing the words about him. I sometimes say words inflict deeper physical pain. Jesus was experiencing both yet in the most painful moments of his life he draws in a deep breath and speaks to the Father knowing the last words he can speak would be words that would set many free. Jesus had every opportunity and right to give in to the hurt and pain; he could have allowed bitterness and hatred to enter his heart because he was innocent. He could have called angels to release him from the pain and shame and show the world who he was. But the love of our Savior for us kept him there.

Luke records this statement, "Jesus said, "Father, forgive them, for they do not know what they are doing." (Luke 23:34 NIV)

We often remember the cross only around the Easter season, and we fail to see how important it is that we remember the cross daily. Every day we must remind ourselves that we too were mockers and scorners of the work of Jesus Christ, we too were in darkness, and walking around blind thinking we knew what was best for us. We were not very different from the mockers at the foot of the cross with the rebellious lifestyles we lived before we met Jesus. The power of the cross to offer forgiveness when we are so undeserving of it cuts to the core of my heart every single time. The cross reminds me that just as I have been so freely forgiven, I can now with the strength of Jesus offer this very same forgiveness to others. My friends we cannot afford to go a day without visiting this place I call the "foot of the cross" because it is here his forgiveness flows freely to all who comes.

Desire: Lord, help me grasp the forgiveness you offer me so I may also offer the same to others.

DAILY SCRIPTURES FOR MEDITATION

Jesus said, "Father, forgive them, for they do not know what they are doing." And they divided up his clothes by casting lots. The people stood watching, and the rulers even sneered at him. They said, "He saved others; let him save himself if he is God's Messiah, the Chosen One." The soldiers also came up and mocked him. They offered him wine vinegar and said, "If you are the king of the Jews, save yourself." - Luke 23:34 – 36 (NIV)

Day 3

At The Cross We Find Freedom

I hope by now you are appreciating the meaning and power of the cross. Today we will look at the aspect of freedom; I often stop and think about prisoners, and as a Pastor, my call and responsibility are to be concerned about the heart condition of all people. I try to spend time every day praying for those who perhaps are forgotten or despised by society because of their actions. I can only imagine a life behind bars day after day, being reminded constantly that the cold steel that keeps them in darkness is the price paid for poor choices made. Never having enough space to move freely, having to use the bathroom with no privacy and the nagging voice of guilt that reminds them of the crime they committed. It sounds treacherous just to imagine it yet every day God's people are behind bars and don't even recognize it.

The bars we live behind are not physical, but they take on the form of spiritual, emotional and mental bars. Some of us have done things in our past we regret, some of us have been abused and carry the scars that keep us from loving or trusting anyone. Maybe even committed unspeakable acts torment us daily. We can't forgive ourselves, and we can't forgive others. No matter what length or height of our bars we all have had them in our lives.

At the foot of the cross, we see two thieves deserving of death because of their choices and crimes. And if we go a step further we can see humanity displayed in these two men. Both being in the presence of the Son of God, seeing and hearing everything from the perspective of Jesus and having the chance to freedom even in death and one stays in rebellion while the other seizes the opportunity to freedom, and to make things right with God before he leaves the earth. Jesus in all his love and mercy offers this unworthy soul grace and freedom from the guilt that plagued him till that point. Today at the foot of the cross you have a choice to break the bars of un-forgiveness, hatred, bitterness, a wretched past, guilt, shame and torment as Jesus offers you the same freedom he offered the thief.

Desire: Lord, help me to accept your freedom; I do not want to be locked up anymore.

DAILY SCRIPTURES FOR MEDITATION

One of the criminals who hung there hurled insults at him: "Aren't you the Messiah? Save yourself and us!" But the other criminal rebuked him. "Don't you fear God," he said, "since you are under the same sentence? We are punished justly, for we are getting what our deeds deserve. But this man has done nothing wrong." Then he said, "Jesus, remember me when you come into your kingdom." Jesus answered him, "Truly I tell you, today you will be with me in paradise." - Luke 23:30-50 (NIV)

He saved us, not because of righteous things we had done, but because of his mercy. He saved us through the washing of rebirth and renewal by the Holy Spirit, whom he poured out on us generously through Jesus Christ our Savior, so that, having been justified by his grace, we might become heirs having the hope of eternal life. Titus 3:5-7 (NIV)

Day 4

At The Cross We Find Family

I often love to look at families with a close bond; I try hard to create a family-pleasing to God. It wasn't always this way for my life as I grew up in a single-parent home and love was the last thing on the agenda of our family. Life was always a hustle and making ends meet, never knowing what it meant to sit around the big family table to enjoy meals together. My mom had to work two jobs, and sometimes I was the helping hands for her. My desire to be part of a loving family never left my heart, and I aspired to create a place where others like me could find the family they never had.

The family is very important to God and has been in his heart since the creation of the earth. The family is the unit that God uses to show us how much he loves us, so the enemy goes after the family unit more than anything else throughout the generations. The enemy knows that a strong family unit will also breed strong communities, so he works overtime to break that bond. One strategy of the enemy is to cause discord and separation because this gives way to the spirit of rejection. When we feel rejected often, we find ourselves in rebellion to those in authority and leadership because of the lack of love from the parent that walked away.

But at the foot of the cross, we see that Jesus in all of his pain and suffering was concerned for the ones he loved especially his mother. He was broken to leave her alone and at that moment provided for her a new son in the Apostle John. That day John also received the greatest honor to care for the mother of the savior of the world. Today you may have experienced the lack of love from your father or mother, perhaps your brothers and sisters have walked away from you, but I want you to know at the cross you become part of a family that transcends blood relatives in the natural realm and you are grafted into a far superior family – The Family of God.

Desire: Lord, help me to appreciate the Royal family I now belong to.

DAILY SCRIPTURES FOR MEDITATION

When Jesus saw his mother there, and the disciple whom he loved standing nearby, he said to her, "Woman, here is your son," and to the disciple, "Here is your mother." From that time on, this disciple took her into his home. - John 19:26-27 (NIV)

For whoever does the will of my Father in heaven is my brother and sister and mother." - Matthew 12:50 (NIV)

The Spirit you received does not make you slaves so that you live in fear again; rather, the Spirit you received brought about your adoption to son ship. And by him, we cry, "Abba, Father." - Romans 8:15 (NIV)

Day 5

At The Cross, The Work Is Finished & We Find Rest

The statement, "The work is finished" is music to my ears. But it is only at the cross we can grasp the concept of Jesus completing the work for us. All my life I desired to please God and I tried desperately to do so without the understanding of the cross. I literally lived life on an emotional rollercoaster. I am sure you can relate to this ride of life. One day I can wake up feeling like I have the power to keep all the rules of the Bible, but after a few days, I slip into the feeling of not being good enough to please God. Sometimes its thoughts that pop into my mind that triggers a guilty feeling or it could be actions contrary to the word, either way; I ended up tired, frustrated and angry that I was not good enough. The truth is we are not good enough within ourselves, and our self-effort will always prove to be futile.

Before the cross man always had to have a substitute for his sins, a lamb that was pure and unblemished had to be presented and sacrificed for the shedding of the blood to atone for sins. This action had to be done year after year after year because the blood of bulls and goats could not complete the work for all time. But when Jesus came to earth he became the perfect lamb that took the place for all mankind because he was the only one that could keep all of God's laws perfectly. Now because of what Jesus did we can come before God in right standing knowing full well we couldn't keep the law but our faith, hope and future rest in the One able to do it. It is the best news I received once I understood the work of the cross. As we come to the end of this plan, I trust that the cross will become part of your daily walk and meditation.

I encourage you to note the following and incorporate them into your quiet times with the Lord. I assure you it will give you strength and renewal each day:

The cross is a place of equality for all men – I have a fair chance.

The cross is a place of revelation – I see the need for a savior.

The cross is a place of repentance – I see the need for a change of mind.

The cross is a place of assurance of redemption – Jesus paid the price.

The cross is a place of salvation – All things can be made new at the foot of the Cross.

Desire: Lord, help me to come to the cross and receive all your free favors

DAILY SCRIPTURES FOR MEDITATION

When he had received the drink, Jesus said, "It is finished." With that, he bowed his head and gave up his spirit. - John 19:30 (NIV)

He did not enter by means of the blood of goats and calves; but he entered the Most Holy Place once for all by his own blood, thus obtaining eternal redemption. The blood of goats and bulls and the ashes of a heifer sprinkled on those who are ceremonially unclean sanctify them so that they are outwardly clean. How much more, then, will the blood of Christ, who through the eternal Spirit offered himself unblemished to God, cleanse our consciences from acts that lead to death, so that we may serve the living God! - Hebrews 9:12-15 (NIV)

"Come to me, all you who are weary and burdened, and I will give you rest. Take my yoke upon you and learn from me, for I am gentle and humble in heart, and you will find rest for your souls. - Matthew 11:28-29 (NIV)

Now that we know what we have—Jesus, this great High Priest with ready access to God—let's not let it slip through our fingers. We don't have a priest who is out of touch with our reality. He's been through weakness and testing, experienced it all—all but the sin. So let's walk right up to him and get what he is so ready to give. Take the mercy, accept the help. - Hebrews 4:15-16 (MSG)

Reflections

Plan 17

THE SILENT BUT DEADLY TRIO

===

Throughout the history of the Bible, the men and women were plagued by what I like to call *the silent but deadly trio.* In today's world, it is no different for us. Everywhere we turn, we are plagued by temptations that "nibble" at our fleshly desires, but the good news is we have been given the remedy to combat the enemy and his tactics.

Day 1

The World System

Have you ever stopped and wondered what drives the world, like what is the modus operandi of this world system? I have pondered this thought a lot in the last couple of years, and from my observation, it can be summed up in this statement, "The pride of life, the lust of the eyes and the lust of the flesh!" Every day the people in the world and that includes believers are presented with this modus operandi. The Apostle John addressed the world system and warned believers to stay away from love for the world. It can become challenging to stay focused in a world so driven by power, achieving, making a name for yourself, technology, advertising, social media, etc. Everything seems to move at warped speed and is readily available at our fingertips. We live in an "instant gratification" world where we have been taught there is no need to wait for anything just order it, and you will have it quickly. While there are places in the world facing significant shortages of food, education, and supplies there seem to be no shortage for feeding the pride and lust of men and women across the earth.

Matthew Henry in his commentary on 1 John 2 stated, "The heart of man is narrow and cannot contain both loves. The world draws down the heart of God, and so the more the love of the world prevails the more the love of God dwindles and decays." Our heart was only made to contain one God whether we serve God the almighty or the god of this world; our life grows from whichever source our heart is connected to.

Forerunner commentary describes worldliness as, "The love of beauty without corresponding love of righteousness" This is a powerful statement as this is made referring to Eve in the Garden of Eden seeing the tree was good for food and was pleasing to the eyes. (Genesis 3:6 NIV). Eve was sucked into the world system of satisfying her desires with no regards for the instruction of her creator. So if this system did not skip Adam and Eve who lived in perfection why do we think it will skip us? As long as the enemy of our soul is on the prowl, we will be subjected to this system but the good news is even though we will be presented with this system of life because of what

Jesus did on the cross for us we are now empowered to live by the system of the kingdom of God. But every day we must be active and alert to the traps of the enemy and make sure we are guarded with the truth of God's love for us and his promises which never fail.

Holy Spirit, open my eyes to see what is in my heart and help me to embrace all of God and His love for me.

DAILY SCRIPTURES FOR MEDITATION

Do not love the world or anything in the world. If anyone loves the world, love for the Father is not in them. For everything in the world—the lust of the flesh, the lust of the eyes, and the pride of life—comes not from the Father but from the world. The world and its desires pass away, but whoever does the will of God lives forever. - 1 John 2:15-17 (NIV)

When the woman saw that the fruit of the tree was good for food and pleasing to the eye, and also desirable for gaining wisdom, she took some and ate it. She also gave some to her husband, who was with her, and he ate it. - Genesis 3:6 (NIV)

Day 2

Products From The World System

The Apostle Paul in his letter to the Romans spoke of life and death and linked both to the mind. While our spirit man is alive and saved when Jesus comes into our hearts at salvation the mind is still our responsibility; the war for the believer is won or lost in the mind. It is amazing that what we act out in life begins in our thoughts. "The mind governed by the flesh is death, but the mind governed by the Spirit is life and peace. The mind governed by the flesh is hostile to God; it does not submit to God's law, nor can it do so. Those who are in the realm of the flesh cannot please God." (Romans 8:6 – 8 NIV). The word flesh in this scripture refers to, "mere human nature, the earthly nature of man apart from divine influence." So whenever we speak of the flesh, we are talking about the thoughts not rooted in righteousness, or have any God kind of influence.

I have heard the saying often while growing up, "You can't stop birds from flying over your head, but you can keep them from making a nest in your hair." – Martin Luther. The enemy may shoot thoughts into our minds, but we need not keep those thoughts and make them our own. The believer now must discern which thoughts are God thoughts and which are from the enemy. The Apostle James explains how sin is conceived by man's own evil desires when he spends time pondering those desires constantly - (James 1:13- 16 NIV). You see because Jesus paid the price for us on the cross and he redeemed us from the curse of sin and death. Now we have the power to grow healthy fruits in our lives based on the choice to have our thoughts governed by the Holy Spirit and God's word by meditating on it daily.

When we give into thoughts that are not godly, we feed those thoughts until they become desires, and then we act out those desires which often leads us to sin. A mind not governed by the word of God, worship, prayer, praise, fellowship with other believers and accountability is a mind very susceptible to the enemy's lies that will eventually destroy. The Apostle Paul used very strong language when warning the saints about evil desires, "Put to death, therefore, whatever belongs to your earthly nature: sexual immorality, impurity, lust, evil desires and greed, which is idolatry." (Colossians 3:5 NIV)

Clearly, we can see from Paul's warning we are responsible for killing those evil desires that will seek to raise its head in our everyday life because it eventually produces idolatry in our lives. It is often said, "We become what we worship" and if our minds are not being governed by the Spirit of God, then we are giving place to idols in our hearts. Nothing good can come from a mind that gives in to every desire. Therefore, understand that the products of the world system will always lead to death while the products of the Spirit will lead to life.

Holy Spirit, give me discernment to identify which thoughts are from you and which are from the enemy. Help me to meditate on your thoughts today.

DAILY SCRIPTURES FOR MEDITATION

Do not love the world or anything in the world. If anyone loves the world, love for the Father is not in them. For everything in the world—the lust of the flesh, the lust of the eyes, and the pride of life—comes not from the Father but from the world. The world and its desires pass away, but whoever does the will of God lives forever. - 1 John 2:15-17 (NIV)

The mind governed by the flesh is death, but the mind governed by the Spirit is life and peace. 7 The mind governed by the flesh is hostile to God; it does not submit to God's law, nor can it do so. 8 Those who are in the realm of the flesh cannot please God. - Romans 8:6-8 (NIV)

When tempted, no one should say, "God is tempting me." For God cannot be tempted by evil, nor does he tempt anyone; but each person is tempted when they are dragged away by their own evil desire and enticed. Then, after desire has conceived, it gives birth to sin; and sin, when it is full-grown, gives birth to death. - James 1:13-15 (NIV)

Put to death, therefore, whatever belongs to your earthly nature: sexual immorality, impurity, lust, evil desires and greed, which is idolatry. - Colossians 3:5 (NIV)

Day 3

Lust Of The Flesh

Often when we hear the statement, "Lust of the flesh" we usually gravitate towards sexual sins only, but lust is so much more than that. The word lust in the Geek is *epithumia*, and it means desire, eagerness for, inordinate desire and lust. The meaning is derived from two words *epi* – which means "focused on" and theymos which mean "passionate desire." When put together we get the definition, "passion build on strong feelings (urges). These can be positive or negative, depending on whether the desire is inspired by faith (God's in birthed persuasion)." From this break down of the word lust, we can see that the source of our focus will lead to our desires. So if we focus on the pressures of this life, images that are sensual, all that is going wrong we will eventually give into anxiety, frustration, sexual immorality, etc. In the same way, if we stay focused on the promises of God like, "My God will supply all my needs" (Philippians 4:19) when financial problems arise we are guaranteed peace and assurance. This is just one example, but God's word has a promise for every situation that may arise in your life. Seek that promise and make sure you keep your mind governed by that word.

The enemy of our soul will continue to look for opportunities to inject the world system into our lives by convincing us that what we want is always "good for us" and know that God's word and instructions are more powerful every time to counteract it. I have heard John Bevere say, "Not every good thing is a God thing." Throughout scriptures from the very beginning, the enemy has used this system until Jesus came and he even tried this same tactic on him but was defeated. Let us look at the lust of the flesh in operation in the lives of a few people in the Old Testament:

1. The enemy approached Eve in the garden and appealed to her flesh by lying to her saying, "The tree was good for food"- (Genesis 3:6a NIV).

2. The enemy fed Sampson the lie that the Philistine woman from Timnah was good for him and he demanded his parents to get her for him as his wife. (Judges 14:2b NIV).

3. The enemy enticed King David to stay at home and be idle when it was a time for the kings to be at war. David got caught satisfying his lust by sleeping with another man's wife named Bathsheba. (2 Samuel 11:4 NIV).

These are just a few examples to show how the lust of the flesh was in operation and again the enemy will always present it in a way to make us believe it is good for us.

Holy Spirit, please give me discernment when gratifying myself. Open up my eyes and mind to ask the question every single time, "Is this a good thing or is this a God thing, will this bring death in the end or will this lead me to live?" Thank you, Holy Spirit for your guidance.

DAILY SCRIPTURES FOR MEDITATION

Do not love the world or anything in the world. If anyone loves the world, love for the Father is not in them. For everything in the world—the lust of the flesh, the lust of the eyes, and the pride of life—comes not from the Father but from the world. The world and its desires pass away, but whoever does the will of God lives forever. - 1 John 2:15-17 (NIV)

And when the woman saw that the tree was good (suitable, pleasant) for food and that it was delightful to look at, and a tree to be desired in order to make one wise, she took of its fruit and ate; and she gave some also to her husband, and he ate. - Genesis 3:6 (AMPC)

Samson went down to Timnah and at Timnah saw one of the daughters of the Philistines.
And he came up and told his father and mother, I saw one of the daughters of the Philistines at Timnah; now get her for me as my wife.

But his father and mother said to him, Is there not a woman among the daughters of your kinsmen or among all our people, that you must go to take a wife from the uncircumcised Philistines? And Samson said to his father, Get her for me, for she is all right in my eyes. - Judges 14:1 – 3 (AMPC)

In the spring, when kings go forth to battle, David sent Joab with his servants and all Israel, and they ravaged the Ammonites [country] and besieged Rabbah. But David remained in Jerusalem.

One evening David arose from his couch and was walking on the roof of the king's house when from there he saw a woman bathing, and she was very lovely to behold.

David sent and inquired about the woman. One said, Is not this Bathsheba, the daughter of Eliam and the wife of Uriah the Hittite?

And David sent messengers and took her. And she came to him, and he lay with her—for she was purified from her uncleanness. Then she returned to her house. - 2 Samuel 11:1-4 (AMPC)

Day 4

Lust Of The Eyes

The lust of the eyes is described as, "the desire to have all that the world offers." We live in a world constantly upgrading and evolving. Gadgets, houses, cars, music, movies, technology, fashion, cosmetic surgery, and the list go on and on. We cannot seem to enjoy what we just purchased because the newer model is always around the corner. Ever changing and time seems to speed along while we try to accumulate what catches our eyes. According to Ron Marshall's article from 2015, it stated, "Digital Marketing Experts estimate that most Americans are exposed to around 4000 to 10,000 advertisements each day" this number is astounding and shows the exposure to the eyes of humans. We obviously don't retain all these images, but this is the tool the enemy seeks to work through because if you have a weakness in a particular area, then the images that appeal to that desire could get locked into your mind and create a focus point.

It makes me ponder, for the believer being exposed to this amount of images daily how much time is needed in getting the God-images into our system. Five minutes a day with the Lord can ever counteract the lust of the eyes. There is a war, and it is won or lost in the mind of man. Let us again look at the three scenarios and individuals from yesterday and see how the lust of the eyes functioned:

1. The enemy appealed to Eve's eyes by ensuring what she was looking at was desirable and delightful, "It was delightful to look at" – (Genesis 3:6b NIV)

2. The enemy again appealed to Samson's eyes by presenting the woman as desirable, and he delighted in what he saw. (Judges 14:1 NIV)

3. The enemy allowed David to walk out on his roof top just at the moment Bathsheba was bathing. David saw her as beautiful and lovely to look at. (2 Samuel 11:2 NIV)

Unfortunately when we allow the images or thoughts not from God to enter through the eye gate and we don't filter it with the lenses of God's word it will get into our minds and eventually into our hearts as we see from the above individuals. It is imperative we filter the images we ponder on as it will determine the fruit we produce.

Holy Spirit, today I desire to guard my eyes. There are so many images presented daily, keep my eyes from wanting everything I see, keep my eyes from pornography and lustful images. Fill my mind with the images for me.

DAILY SCRIPTURES FOR MEDITATION

Do not love the world or anything in the world. If anyone loves the world, love for the Father is not in them. For everything in the world—the lust of the flesh, the lust of the eyes, and the pride of life—comes not from the Father but from the world. The world and its desires pass away, but whoever does the will of God lives forever. - 1 John 2:15-17 (NIV)

And when the woman saw that the tree was good (suitable, pleasant) for food and that it was delightful to look at, and a tree to be desired in order to make one wise, she took of its fruit and ate; and she gave some also to her husband, and he ate. - Genesis 3:6 (AMPC)

Samson went down to Timnah and at Timnah saw one of the daughters of the Philistines.
And he came up and told his father and mother; I saw one of the daughters of the Philistines at Timnah; now get her for me as my wife.
But his father and mother said to him, Is there not a woman among the daughters of your kinsmen or among all our people, that you must go to take a wife from the uncircumcised Philistines? And Samson said to his father, Get her for me, for she is all right in my eyes. - Judges 14:1 – 3 (AMPC)

In the spring, when kings go forth to battle, David sent Joab with his servants and all Israel, and they ravaged the Ammonites [country] and besieged Rabbah. But David remained in Jerusalem.
One evening David arose from his couch and was walking on the roof

of the king's house when from there he saw a woman bathing, and she was very lovely to behold.

David sent and inquired about the woman. One said, Is not this Bathsheba, the daughter of Eliam and the wife of Uriah the Hittite? And David sent messengers and took her. And she came into him, and he lay with her—for she was purified from her uncleanness. Then she returned to her house. - 2 Samuel 11:1-4 (AMPC)

Day 5

The Pride Of Life

Pride is described as the "desire of the world's approval rather than the approval of God." This proves to be very true because everyday life seems to be a competition for approval from our peers, business associates and in the end we long to hear the praise of men while forgetting our creator. The Apostle John also described it this way, "the pride of life [assurance in one's own resources or in the stability of earthly things]—these do not come from the Father but are from the world [itself]." (1 John 2:16b AMPC). Pride can hide itself and can be very subtle, I think we all have a measure of pride hidden deep within; nothing is wrong in celebrating success and enjoying the finer things in life, but when it borders on us taking the credit for the success and pay no mind to God or show thankfulness and gratitude we are then rooted in pride.

Pride is most dangerous in the world's system because pride makes a statement. "I don't need God because I know what is best for me and I can control my life and my future." Lucifer the archangel created by God in beauty and splendor and was in charge of worship in heaven was found with pride, and he desired to be in the place of God. Lucifer's fall from heaven was because of pride, see (Isaiah 14:12-17, Ezekiel 28:13-17 NIV).

Let us again examine the individuals' lives we've been following for the past two days as the pride of life ruled them:

1. The enemy appealed to Eve's pride by enticing her with the lie she would become wise and like God, "And a tree to be desired in order to make one wise, she took of its fruit and ate; and she gave some also to her husband, and he ate. (Genesis 3:6c NIV)

2. The enemy again appealed to Sampson's pride by allowing him to believe he knew what was best for him, "And Samson said to his father, Get her for me, for she is all right in my eyes." (Judges 14:3b NIV)

3. The enemy appealed to David's pride by causing him to use his position as King to bypass accountability and allowed him to

believe that as King he could do as he please, "And David sent messengers and took her. And she came to him, and he lay with her." (2 Samuel 11:4a NIV)

All three individuals were presented with something or someone that would promise satisfaction to their immediate desires. All focused on the object or person until they burned with desire or had a strong urge to have it. All convinced themselves that it was good for them and ultimately gave in. Eve's decision to give in to the world system brought death to all creation, Samson lost his eyes and was imprisoned and treated like an animal, and King David committed adultery and murder because of his choice. While they were redeemed from their sins because of Jesus, they all suffered a huge cost and the products of their actions will be remembered forever. While this may all sound hopeless for us, I don't want you to be discouraged, because of Jesus we need not give in to the world system.

Holy Spirit, please help me to recognize the subtly of pride in my life. Help me to weigh the cost of my choices and decisions and help me to remember Eve, Sampson, and King David regularly as I ponder life.

DAILY SCRIPTURES FOR MEDITATION

Do not love the world or anything in the world. If anyone loves the world, love for the Father is not in them. For everything in the world—the lust of the flesh, the lust of the eyes, and the pride of life—comes not from the Father but from the world. The world and its desires pass away, but whoever does the will of God lives forever. - 1 John 2:15-17 (NIV)

And when the woman saw that the tree was good (suitable, pleasant) for food and that it was delightful to look at, and a tree to be desired in order to make one wise, she took of its fruit and ate; and she gave some also to her husband, and he ate. - Genesis 3:6 (AMPC)

Samson went down to Timnah and at Timnah saw one of the daughters of the Philistines.

And he came up and told his father and mother, I saw one of the daughters of the Philistines at Timnah; now get her for me as my wife. But his father and mother said to him, Is there not a woman among the daughters of your kinsmen or among all our people, that you must go to take a wife from the uncircumcised Philistines? And Samson said to his father, Get her for me, for she is all right in my eyes. - Judges 14:1 – 3 (AMPC)

In the spring, when kings go forth to battle, David sent Joab with his servants and all Israel, and they ravaged the Ammonites [country] and besieged Rabbah. But David remained in Jerusalem.
One evening David arose from his couch and was walking on the roof of the king's house when from there he saw a woman bathing; and she was very lovely to behold.
David sent and inquired about the woman. One said, Is not this Bathsheba, the daughter of Eliam and the wife of Uriah the Hittite?
And David sent messengers and took her. And she came into him, and he lay with her—for she was purified from her uncleanness. Then she returned to her house. - 2 Samuel 11:1-4 (AMPC)

How you have fallen from heaven, morning star, son of the dawn! You have been cast down to the earth, you who once laid low the nations! You said in your heart, "I will ascend to the heavens; I will raise my throne   above the stars of God; I will sit enthroned on the mount of assembly, on the utmost heights of Mount Zaphon.
I will ascend above the tops of the clouds;   I will make myself like the Most High." But you are brought down to the realm of the dead, to the depths of the pit. - Isaiah 14:12-15 (NIV)

You were in Eden, the garden of God; every precious stone adorned you: carnelian, chrysolite, and emerald, topaz, onyx, and jasper, lapis lazuli, turquoise, and beryl. Your settings and mountings were made of gold; on the day you were created they were prepared. You were anointed as a guardian cherub, for so I ordained you. You were on the holy mount of God; you walked among the fiery stones. You were blameless in your ways from the day you were created till wickedness was found in you. - Ezekiel 28:13-15 (NIV)

Pride goes before destruction and a haughty spirit before a fall. -

Proverbs 16:18 (AMPC)

Day 6

It Is Written

Until Jesus came, it was difficult for anyone to beat the world system of the "Lust of the flesh, lust of the eyes and the pride of life." But today I am so grateful that Jesus not only beat the system, but he enabled us to do the same by giving us his Spirit to indwell us. The help given to us in the person of the Holy Spirit is amazing if we learn how to host him and keep our minds governed by him. The Bible tells us clearly that Jesus, once he was baptized by John and he came up out of the water, the heavens opened, and the Holy Spirit rested on Jesus, and then he was led into the wilderness to fast and pray for forty days to be tested. (Matthew 4:1-11 NIV)

The enemies of our souls have employed this world system from the beginning of time and will continue to enforce it till the end; this system didn't skip the men and women of old, it did not skip Jesus, and it sure won't skip us. But we must become wise by spending time with the Holy Spirit; reading and meditating on the word, praising and worshiping because this habit is the only way to beat the world system. Let us examine the temptations presented to Jesus and see how he counteracted it:

1. After forty days Jesus was hungry, and the enemy appealed to the need of Jesus flesh at that moment to satisfy his hunger, the enemy said to him, "If you are the Son of God, tell these stones to become bread." (Matthew 4:3b NIV). Jesus immediately responds with an "it is written statement." "It is written: 'Man shall not live by bread alone, but on every word that comes from the mouth of God.'" (Matthew 4:4 NIV)

2. The enemy appealed to Jesus' pride by telling him to prove his power and authority as the Son of God. "If you are the Son of God," he said, "throw yourself down. For it is written:

"'He will command his angels concerning you, and they will lift you up in their hands so that you will not strike your foot against a stone. '" Again Jesus responds with the word of God, "Jesus answered him, "It is also written: 'Do not put the Lord your God to the test.'"

(Matthew 4:5-7 NIV)

3. The enemy tries one more time by appealing to the eyes; showing him all he could gain if he would just bow down and worship Satan. "All this I will give you," he said, "if you will bow down and worship me." (Matthew 4:9 NIV). And Jesus immediately shuts him up by responding, "Away from me, Satan! For it is written: 'Worship the Lord your God, and serve him only.'" (Matthew 4:10b NIV).

Jesus single-handedly decimated the world system by having the written word in his heart, mind, and mouth. There is no other way to defeat the enemy and his system except by habitually walking and living by the Spirit of God.

Holy Spirit, I welcome you to walk and talk with me daily. Manifest your power in my life so I may overcome the world system just like Jesus did.

DAILY SCRIPTURES FOR MEDITATION

Do not love the world or anything in the world. If anyone loves the world, love for the Father is not in them. For everything in the world—the lust of the flesh, the lust of the eyes, and the pride of life—comes not from the Father but from the world. The world and its desires pass away, but whoever does the will of God lives forever. - 1 John 2:15-17 (NIV)

Then Jesus was led by the Spirit into the wilderness to be tempted by the devil. After fasting forty days and forty nights, he was hungry. The tempter came to him and said, "If you are the Son of God, tell these stones to become bread." Jesus answered, "It is written: 'Man shall not live by bread alone, but on every word that comes from the mouth of God.'" Then the devil took him to the holy city and had him stand on the highest point of the temple. "If you are the Son of God," he said, "throw yourself down. For it is written: '"He will command his angels concerning you, and they will lift you up in their hands so that you will not strike your foot against a stone."'"
Jesus answered him, "It is also written: 'Do not put the Lord your God to the test.'" Again, the devil took him to a very high mountain and

showed him all the kingdoms of the world and their splendor. "All this I will give you," he said, "if you will bow down and worship me." Jesus said to him, "Away from me, Satan! For it is written: 'Worship the Lord your God, and serve him only.'" Then the devil left him, and angels came and attended him. - Matthew 4:1-11 (NIV)

So I say, walk by the Spirit, and you will not gratify the desires of the flesh. For the flesh desires what is contrary to the Spirit, and the Spirit what is contrary to the flesh. They are in conflict with each other so that you are not to do whatever you want. But if you are led by the Spirit, you are not under the law. The acts of the flesh are obvious: sexual immorality, impurity, and debauchery; idolatry and witchcraft; hatred, discord, jealousy, fits of rage, selfish ambition, dissensions, factions and envy; drunkenness, orgies, and the like. I warn you, as I did before, that those who live like this will not inherit the kingdom of God. - Galatians 5:16-21 (NIV)

Reflections

_____
_____
_____
_____
_____
_____
_____
_____
_____
_____
_____
_____
_____
_____
_____
_____
_____
_____
_____
_____
_____
_____
_____
_____

Plan 18

THE VALUE OF TIME

===

Have you ever pondered the meaning of "time" and the importance of it? We all know that time is precious, but do we live life valuing time? In this devotional, you will gain an understanding of how precious time is for the believer and try to use your time wisely.

Day 1

The Beginning Of Time

Have you ever wondered when time began? What is this concept of time? Who created time?

I never paid much attention to this topic until I was preparing a sermon series for church and God spoke to my heart about time. The answer is God created time, and it did not happen by some random big bang! The Bible opens up with the whole concept of time, in the book of Genesis it speaks of God coming onto the scene of total darkness, emptiness, and nothingness. It tells us of the Holy Spirit brooding over this murky scene, and then God spoke his first recorded words, "Let there be light; and there was light." (Genesis 1:5 NIV).

After God spoke light into existence, he saw it was good, and God distinguished between light and darkness and this marked the beginning of time.

From this understanding of the beginning of time, it will stand to reason, there must also be an end to time. I present to you today that time is a gift from God and we must learn to value the time we have been given.

What are you spending your time on today and is it adding or taking away from your life?

Prayer: Help me Lord to understand the gift of time.

DAILY SCRIPTURES FOR MEDITATION

In the beginning, God (prepared, formed, fashioned, and) created the heavens and the earth. The earth was without form and an empty waste, and darkness was upon the face of the very great deep. The Spirit of God was moving (hovering, brooding) over the face of the waters. And God said, Let there be light, and there was light. And God saw that the light was good (suitable, pleasant) and He approved it; and God separated the light from the darkness.
And God called the light Day, and the darkness He called Night. And there was evening, and there was morning, one day. - Genesis 1:1-5 Amplified Bible (AMPC)

Day 2

Defining Time

Yesterday we looked at the beginning of time, and we reasoned that if there is a beginning to time, there must be an end. The Apostle Peter presents to us that time will end when the day of the Lord appears. When Jesus returns to rule and reign forever time as we know it will end. He explains that everything we see around us and the world as we know it will dissolve and be destroyed by fire. He encourages us not to be so focused on the material things of this world because as time draws to a close, all will be destroyed.

In the book of Revelation, the Apostle John talks about the new heaven and the new earth where there will be no night, and the Lord will be all the light we need.

Wayne Jackson, in his article from Christiancourier.com, defines time this way, "Perhaps another way to explain it is to suggest that "time" is a historical parenthesis within eternity." The fact is time appears minuscule compared to eternity, and this comparison gives more weight to the teaching of Jesus when he said, "What good is it for a man to gain the whole world but lose his own soul" (Matthew 16:26 NIV). Every day people are working long hours to build a life of material possessions while forgetting the time we have on earth is as it suggests only for a short period.

Psalm 90 is a recorded prayer of Moses where he identifies the approximate span of years given to man to be between 70 or 80 years. When we take the whole picture of eternity and you in context it could be summarized like this:

Eternity = Forever

Time = historical parenthesis within eternity (civilization approx. 6000 – 10,000 years)

You = 70 – 80 years within time (a drop in the bucket)

Selah – pause and think about it!

With this new understanding you have gained on time, what will you do differently today with your time?

Prayer: Help Me Lord to value my time

DAILY SCRIPTURES FOR MEDITATION

But the day of the Lord will come like a thief. The heavens will disappear with a roar; the elements will be destroyed by fire, and the earth and everything done in it will be laid bare. Since everything will be destroyed in this way, what kind of people ought you to be? You ought to live holy and godly lives as you look forward to the day of God and speed its coming. That day will bring about the destruction of the heavens by fire, and the elements will melt in the heat. - 2 Peter 3:10-12 (NIV)

There will be no more night. They will not need the light of a lamp or the light of the sun, for the Lord God will give them light. And they will reign for ever and ever. - Revelation 22:5 (NIV)

What good will it be for someone to gain the whole world, yet forfeit their soul? Or what can anyone give in exchange for their soul? - Matthew 16:26 (NIV)

Our days may come to seventy years, or eighty, if our strength endures; yet the best of them are but trouble and sorrow, for they quickly pass, and we fly away. - Psalm 90:10 (NIV)

Day 3

Valuing Time Births Wisdom

When you take a view of your life compared to eternity, it causes you to become sober-minded. Thomas Edison said, "Time is really the only capital that any human being has, and the only thing he can't afford to lose." Many people think that more money will make them more valuable and wise, but the truth is when you learn to value the capital (time) you have been given then you are on the path to becoming wise. When we learn to value time we are learning to value our lives and those around us.

Imagine daily people are scurrying around using their time to accumulate wealth and riches while their families are neglected, their children go off on the wrong path and their health suffers. Jim Rohn said, "Time is of more value than money, you can get more money, but you cannot get more time." Once time is gone, we can't get it back so today I want to encourage you to become wise by not compromising your relationships and health in the chase of unnecessary material possessions. Be a present mom or dad using your time to create memories with your family that would outlive you! Invest the capital of time into strong, godly foundations for your family by making time to go to church together, maybe watch a family movie, or even have meals around the table. Invest time in listening to the ones you love because one day you will want them to listen to you.

The Lord Jesus said, " For where your treasure is, there your heart will be also." Matthew 6:21 (NIV). Our hearts follow our treasure; I pray today you would treasure the capital of time and invest it wisely because once it is gone, you cannot get it back.

Prayer: Lord, give me a heart of wisdom so I can govern my time.

DAILY SCRIPTURES FOR MEDITATION

Teach us to number our days, that we may gain a heart of wisdom. - Psalm 90:12 (NIV)

"Show me, Lord, my life's end. and the number of my days; let me know how fleeting my life is. - Psalm 39:4 (NIV)

But store up for yourselves treasures in heaven, where moths and vermin do not destroy, and where thieves do not break in and steal. For where your treasure is, there your heart will be also. - Matthew 6:20-22 (NIV)

Day 4

Valuing Time Leads To The Redemption Of Lost Time

While preparing my sermon on time in 2015, I came across this headline in The Huffington Post, "You Can Determine What You Value by Where You Spend Your Time" written by Scott Anderson. The statement caught my attention, and I spent time just pondering on it. I realized that time is a currency which we invest and whatever we invest our time in will also bring a return be it good or bad rewards. When we gain wisdom that time is so short compared to eternity the words of God, the instructions of God has a new value. Recognize that time invested in God's plans and purposes for us will only bring the best rewards. When we value the time, we can actually redeem lost and wasted years.

The Apostle Paul in writing to the Church in Ephesus encouraged the saints to live in obedience to God's words because the times they were living in was full of deceptions of the soul. It was much like our times, and he was warning them that the choices or decisions they make could either steal their time away from the kingdom or they could redeem the lost time.

Every time we make a choice to follow God's way we are obeying his will for our lives, and that frees up more time for us to accomplish more for him. We can actually do more for the kingdom when we need not keep cleaning up the messes of our poor choices.

I value time more now that I am older because I realized the years left are but a few, but when I was in my twenties I thought I had all the time in the world, and that led to so many destructive decisions in my life. I want to encourage you today to look at the choices and the decisions you are making daily and take stock of how much you value time.

Prayer: Lord, help me today to make better choices and decisions so I can redeem the lost time.

DAILY SCRIPTURES FOR MEDITATION

For He knows our frame, He [earnestly] remembers and imprints [on

His heart] that we are dust. As for man, his days are as grass; as a flower of the field, so he flourishes. For the wind passes over it and it is gone, and its place shall know it no more. But the mercy and loving-kindness of the Lord are from everlasting to everlasting upon those who reverently and worshipfully fear him, and His righteousness is to children's children— To such as keep His covenant [hearing, receiving, loving, and obeying it] and to those who [earnestly] remember His commandments to do them [imprinting them on their hearts]. - Psalm 103:14-18 (AMP)

For you were once darkness, but now you are light in the Lord. Live as children of light (for the fruit of the light consists in all goodness, righteousness and truth) and find out what pleases the Lord. Have nothing to do with the fruitless deeds of darkness, but rather expose them. It is shameful even to mention what the disobedient do in secret. But everything exposed by the light becomes visible—and everything that is illuminated becomes a light. This is why it is said: "Wake up, sleeper, rise from the dead, and Christ will shine on you." Be very careful, then, how you live—not as unwise but as wise, making the most of every opportunity, because the days are evil. Therefore do not be foolish, but understand what the Lord's will is. - Ephesians 5:8-16 (NIV)

So watch your step. Use your head. Make the most of every chance you get. These are desperate times! - Ephesians 5:16 (MSG)

Day 5

Time Stealer

There will always be distractions in life because we know from scripture that the agenda of the enemy is to steal, kill and destroy - (John 10:10 NIV). Because of his agenda to steal from us, the enemy knows if we can waste time then our purpose will never be realized, and our destiny will be aborted.

Procrastination is a time stealer, and it simply means to put off intentionally doing something that should be done

I have been guilty of this often, and I have missed many wonderful opportunities to excel. In the Bible, (Matthew 25:1 – 13 NIV), a story of procrastination gripped my heart because of the greatest opportunity missed. The parable of the ten virgins tells of the preparation for the bridegroom's return. Five of the virgins were prepared with their lamps and oil, but five did not have oil. The story points out that the bridegroom was a long time in coming and the virgins became drowsy and fell asleep. Then suddenly at midnight, the alarm was sounded that the bridegroom was on his way. They all awoke, and the five prepared put their lamps together for his return. But the five who had sufficient time but intentionally put off getting the oil was left stranded and never made it to the wedding.

This parable was a real eye-opener for me because I realize every day we are gambling away our future with the notion we still have lots of time while being distracted by unimportant things like social media, television, games, text messages and the list can go on. Today I want to encourage you to look at what you are investing your time in and ask yourself, "What am I putting off intentionally that could hurt my future that I should be doing right now?" Once you have identified it simply decide not to put it off anymore; redeem your time!

Prayer: Lord, help me today to not be like the five virgins that gambled with their future. Help me to break off this time stealer of procrastination from my life and thank you for your hearing me!

DAILY SCRIPTURES FOR MEDITATION

"At that time the kingdom of heaven will be like ten virgins who took their lamps and went out to meet the bridegroom. Five of them were foolish, and five were wise. The foolish ones took their lamps but did not take any oil with them. The wise ones, however, took oil in jars along with their lamps. The bridegroom was a long time in coming, and they all became drowsy and fell asleep. - Matthew 25:1 - 5 (NIV)

"At midnight the cry rang out: 'Here's the bridegroom! Come out to meet him!' "Then all the virgins woke up and trimmed their lamps. The foolish ones said to the wise, 'Give us some of your oil; our lamps are going out.' "'No,' they replied, 'there may not be enough for both us and you. Instead, go to those who sell oil and buy some for yourselves.' "But while they were on their way to buy the oil, the bridegroom arrived. The virgins who were ready went in with him to the wedding banquet. And the door was shut. - Matthew 25:6 - 10 (NIV)

"Later the others also came. 'Lord, Lord,' they said, 'open the door for us!' "But he replied, 'Truly I tell you, I don't know you.' "Therefore keep watch, because you do not know the day or the hour. - Matthew 25:11 - 13 (NIV)

Reflections

_____
_____
_____
_____
_____
_____
_____
_____
_____
_____
_____
_____
_____
_____
_____
_____
_____
_____
_____
_____
_____
_____
_____
_____
_____

Plan 19

WAITING ON THE LORD

==

"Waiting"- I don't know about you, but I become irate when I must wait. It's at this time I realize just how low my patience level is. As children of God, it sometimes becomes even more frustrating when we must wait for something we have been praying for because God the Father has tremendous patience and it's a characteristic he wants each of us to develop. Waiting can be our friend, or it can be our foe, it can be positive or negative, it can be joyous, or it can be full of sorrow; ultimately the choice is yours.

Day 1

A People In Waiting

Waiting sounds drawn out and like a very dull process. In this ever moving and evolving culture, waiting is a thing of the past. Technology has put us on the cutting edge of optimization so we don't even have to go physically to an interview; it can be conducted over a computer screen, or we can have food delivered right to our doorsteps by using an app cutting out human interaction on the phone, and there is an app for almost everything we need today. Even our parents and grandparents have cell phones and apps. I am not against technology, optimization, and strategies that make people's lives easier; my concern is the inability to wait on anything breeding impatience, frustrations, and anxiety. One area I notice a lot of impatience and anger evident is while driving, we are in such a hurry, and if someone pauses a minute too long when a stoplight turns green, the horns will be honking.

Patience is a virtue that our God majors in, there is no one more patient than him, and we see that trait flowing throughout the pages of his word. I am sure God would love to return, and swoop his people up in his big burly arms and shower us with all his love, but his love keeps him from coming just yet because there are many of his children he is still waiting on to come home. While we may not like to wait, patience is a fruit of the Spirit and should be exercised in the life of every believer. How about you? Do you like to wait? What is your patience level? Which area of your life are you struggling with being patient? Ever so often we should stop and take stock of our lives because sometimes we can go off the track and don't even recognize it.

We are all a people in waiting, every day we must wait in line at the grocery, bus stop, train station, in traffic, or wait on a phone call, text message, or wait on our kids, wait for the shower, or wait for our dinner. It doesn't matter our age, color, height, or weight we are all a people in waiting, but how we view the waiting process will eventually determine the day, week, month, year, and the life we will have. Waiting can be our friend, or it can be our foe, it can be positive or negative, it can be joyous, or it can be full of sorrow; ultimately the choice is yours. I pray as you read through this plan, you will view the waiting process as a "God Thing" which will eventually turn into a "Good Thing."

> *"If the Lord Jehovah makes us wait, let us do so with our whole hearts; for blessed are all they that wait for Him. He is worth waiting for. The waiting itself is beneficial to us: it tries faith, exercises patience, trains submission, and endears the blessing when it comes. The Lord's people have always been a waiting people" - Charles Spurgeon.*

DAILY SCRIPTURES FOR MEDITATION

But those who hope in the Lord will renew their strength. They will soar on wings like eagles; they will run and not grow weary, they will walk and not be faint. - Isaiah 40:31 (NIV)

Be still before the Lord. and wait patiently for him; do not fret when people succeed in their ways, when they carry out their wicked schemes. - Psalm 37:7 (NIV)

Trust in the Lord with all your heart. And lean not on your own understanding; in all your ways submit to him, and he will make your paths straight. - Proverbs 3:5-6 (NIV)

But the fruit of the [Holy] Spirit [the work which His presence within accomplishes] is love, joy (gladness), peace, patience (an even temper, forbearance), kindness, goodness (benevolence), faithfulness, Gentleness (meekness, humility), self-control (self-restraint, continence). Against such things, there is no law [[a]that can bring a charge]. - Galatians 5:22-23 (AMPC)

The Lord is not slow in keeping his promise, as some understand slowness. Instead, he is patient with you, not wanting anyone to perish, but everyone to come to repentance. - 2 Peter 3:9 (NIV)

Day 2

Waiting Is Always Connected To A Promise

When waiting, it means we have an expectation, and we anticipate a wonderful end, but this end was based on a promise we received. The promise we receive is both a seed and a harvest. When we first get a promise, it is actually in seed form, and then we must wait a while before we can see that seed turn into a harvest hence the reason for the waiting process. Our waiting is based on an expectation of the seed turning into a harvest.

A mother expects a baby after she gets the news she is pregnant, and she then gets excited. She eats carefully, she thinks about the color of the baby's room, and though her tummy is still flat, she now has a hope and expectation for the end result. When a woman gets engaged, her ring is the seed that the harvest of marriage is coming, and she starts with great anticipation to prepare the way in advance for the happy ever after with the perfect guy. When a man is granted his first business loan, it is the seed he will one day reap a harvest of owning a multimillion dollar corporation. So you see everything we are waiting on began with a seed.

In life sometimes we lose track of the promise, and when we do our waiting process becomes hard, long, laborious, and frustrating. We blame God for the delay, and we can even become rebellious towards God and the people we do life with. The bible tells us there is seed time and there is harvest time, and this suggests that between the seed and the harvest, there is the thing called "TIME." Maybe you are in this place where you are losing faith, growing weary, and frustrated and you feel like running ahead of God, but I want to encourage you to hold on, go back to the promise God gave you in seed form and envision the harvest. What does it look like? What were your desires, dreams, and vision when God gave you the seed?

Take a few moments today meditating on the seed God gave you and see hope arise again, God is good on his promises, and he will never fail you even though it may be taking longer than you expected. Many people give up halfway; they turn their backs on their dreams and vision because they became hopeless. Hope helps us carry on when life gets rough; to hope means to have a joyful, confident expectation of good and the only way we can maintain hope is by holding on to the promises of God. The main reason people take their lives is that they were convinced all hope was gone and the enemy loves to keep people hopeless. Our God is a God of hope so, please go back to your promise and be revived again!

Hope is called the anchor of the soul (Hebrews 6:19) because it gives stability to the Christian life. But hope is not simply a 'wish' (I wish that such-and-such would take place); rather, it is that which latches onto the certainty of the promises of the future that God has made. - RC Sproul

DAILY SCRIPTURES FOR MEDITATION

But those who hope in the Lord will renew their strength. They will soar on wings like eagles; they will run and not grow weary, they will walk and not be faint. - Isaiah 40:31 (NIV)

While the earth remains, seedtime and harvest, cold and heat, summer and winter, and day and night shall not cease. - Genesis 8:22 (AMPC)

Return to the stronghold [of security and prosperity], you prisoners of hope; even today do I declare that I will restore double your former prosperity to you. - Zechariah 9:12 (AMPC)

The Lord is not slow in keeping his promise, as some understand slowness. Instead, he is patient with you, not wanting anyone to perish, but everyone to come to repentance. - 2 Peter 3:9 (NIV)

Day 3

Inability To Wait Will Give Birth To Long-term Chaos And Confusion

As we learned yesterday, waiting is always connected to a promise. Today we will look at what happens when we are not willing to wait on the Lord. I love the life of Abraham because he seemed like the most down to earth guy that ever lived even though he was chosen and favored by God. When I am down, I like to read about Abraham because the story of his life infuses me with hope to carry on, but I also get to see the humanity, frailty, and simplicity of a man just like me. Abraham was called a man of great faith, but he had flaws and lying was one. He was fearful hence the reason for his lying, he had doubts about God's promises, and he gave in to temptation, yet, God blessed him long before he made his mistakes.

Today, because of Jesus we are also chosen and blessed even with all our flaws, but if we go ahead of God's promise and cut our waiting period short, the consequences of that action will still manifest and are ours to deal with. God's promises contain the best for us and when we bypass the process of waiting we give up the best for less.

Abraham received a promise he would have a son of his own but time was going by, and nothing seemed to happen, and Abraham went to the Lord full of doubts and fears because he had no children. He was getting old, and his inheritance would have to be left for his servant. God reassured Abraham he would have a son of his own – "Then the word of the Lord came to him: "This man will not be your heir, but a son who is your own flesh and blood will be your heir." (Genesis 15:4 NIV). Abraham pressed on to believe, but his wife Sarah was running out of patience because she also was old and passed the stage of childbearing. It seemed like their lives were wasting away. They had followed God's instructions and left their homeland in search of the promise of God, yet the one thing they desired most was taking the longest. Are you in a place like this? Are all the natural circumstances shouting that God has forgotten you, and get up and help yourself achieve the promise faster?

Sarah didn't want to wait because she looked at herself and her age and thought, "Surely this child is not going to come from my body so let me see if I can give Abraham a little help in moving the process along, after all, God only told Abraham the son would come from his own body, so maybe this doesn't need me." And like any wife who has lost their natural and spiritual mind, she offers Abraham her maid to sleep with – "so she said to Abram, "The Lord has kept me from having children. Go, sleep with my slave; perhaps I can build a family through her." (Genesis 16:2 NIV). What? As you read this, it sounds absurd, but when we are not willing to wait, we will find ourselves resorting to desperate means and measures to fulfill a promise only God can fulfill. Due to their inability to wait on the promise, chaos broke out in the home after the maid got pregnant, a son was born out of human intervention, and till today the struggle ensues between the people that came from the maid and the people that came from the promise. Is it worth the risk to move ahead of God? Today I pray that if the thought of giving up or trying your own way is bombarding you, that you will take time and ask God for help to wait on him.

"The cure for impatience with the fulfillment of God's timetable is to believe His promises, obey His will, and leave the results to Him. So often when God's timetable stretches into years, we become discouraged and...want to give up or try to work something out on [our] own." - Jerry Bridges

DAILY SCRIPTURES FOR MEDITATION

But those who hope in the Lord will renew their strength. They will soar on wings like eagles; they will run and not grow weary, they will walk and not be faint. - Isaiah 40:31 (NIV)

The Lord is not slow in keeping his promise, as some understand slowness. Instead, he is patient with you, not wanting anyone to perish, but everyone to come to repentance. - 2 Peter 3:9 (NIV)

Day 4

Inability To Wait Will Bring Bondage, Blindness, And Confinement

Today we will look at the life of another great man in the bible whose inability to wait cost him dearly. He was perfect in bodily structure and strength, but his ego was too big to be contained. He was emotional and passionate, smart, but very self-centered. He had a great call on his life, but he had no patience. His name is Sampson and while God's hand was upon his life, and he did great feats in his life, and even in death, his inability to wait on the lord cut his life and purpose short. Like Abraham, Sampson was chosen by God to be a Judge and a warrior for Israel and his physical strength was immaculate, he had no match. The instructions given to Sampson's parents were very precise from God because his call was huge. It was to defend and protect his nation from the Philistines – "You will become pregnant and have a son whose head is never to be touched by a razor because the boy is to be a Nazirite, dedicated to God from the womb. He will take the lead in delivering Israel from the hands of the Philistines." (Judges 13:5 NIV).

Everything was observed, and Sampson grew in strength and stature, but his inability to wait caused him to live life by the flesh, and he sought to satisfy his every desire. One day he saw a young Philistine woman he liked and demanded his parents to get her for him even though it was forbidden, but God had a plan to use it all for his purpose. No one could defeat Sampson, and that sent the Philistines on a quest to figure out the source of his strength since they couldn't defeat him with physical strength; they realized he had a weakness for women, and they used the women in Sampson's life to manipulate him. Sampson epitomizes the dual sides of us as humans; we can be very strong in some areas of our lives and have a deadly weakness. The Bible tells us the enemy goes about like a roaring lion seeking whom he may devour – "Be alert and of sober mind. Your enemy, the devil, prowls around like a roaring lion looking for someone to devour." (1 Peter 5:8). The enemy studies us, he sits and is very patient to watch our every move, and once he figures out our weakness, then he plots our downfall. The problem comes in when we believe we are so strong we need not take precautions for our weak areas.

Sampson had many ups and downs in his life, but at every juncture, he had victory until he finally gave away the secret of his strength in his weakest moment, he shared his secret with Delilah. More than one time he tricked Delilah by giving her the wrong information, and he knew she was giving away the secrets to the enemy yet he continued to satisfy his flesh until the truth of his secret was revealed. Sampson told Delilah his strength was in his hair and that brought his demise. He was captured, and his eyes were gouged out, and now he would become a show for the Philistines because his strength was gone. He was used as an animal to ground at the mill in their prison. Had Sampson learned to wait on the Lord I believe he would have done greater things and lived longer, but he didn't know how to wait. When we refuse to wait on the Lord, we too can grope around in the dark, being bound and subjected to people's opinions, and bound to the control of men and women. Even though Sampson's hair grew back and he eventually defeated the enemy it also cost him his life. I encourage you to weigh carefully what hangs in the balance in your "waiting" process and trust God to come through for you.

"A Christian without patience is like a soldier without arms." - *Thomas Watson*

DAILY SCRIPTURES FOR MEDITATION

But those who hope in the Lord will renew their strength. They will soar on wings like eagles; they will run and not grow weary, they will walk and not be faint. - Isaiah 40:31 (NIV)

Samson went down to Timnah and saw there a young Philistine woman. When he returned, he said to his father and mother, "I have seen a Philistine woman in Timnah; now get her for me as my wife." His father and mother replied, "Isn't there an acceptable woman among your relatives or among all our people? Must you go to the uncircumcised Philistines to get a wife?"
But Samson said to his father, "Get her for me. She's the right one for me." - Judges 14:1-3 (NIV)

With such nagging, she prodded him day after day until he was sick to death of it.

So he told her everything. "No razor has ever been used on my head," he said, "because I have been a Nazirite dedicated to God from my mother's womb. If my head were shaved, my strength would leave me, and I would become as weak as any other man."

When Delilah saw that he had told her everything, she sent word to the rulers of the Philistines, "Come back once more; he has told me everything." So the rulers of the Philistines returned with the silver in their hands. After putting him to sleep on her lap, she called for someone to shave off the seven braids of his hair, and so began to subdue him. And his strength left him.

Then she called, "Samson, the Philistines are upon you!"

He awoke from his sleep and thought, "I'll go out as before and shake myself free." But he did not know that the Lord had left him.

Then the Philistines seized him, gouged out his eyes and took him down to Gaza. Binding him with bronze shackles, they set him to grinding grain in the prison. But the hair on his head began to grow again after it had been shaved. - Judges 16:16-21 (NIV)

Now the rulers of the Philistines assembled to offer a great sacrifice to Dagon, their god and to celebrate, saying, "Our god has delivered Samson, our enemy, into our hands." When the people saw him, they praised their god, saying, "Our god has delivered our enemy   into our hands, the one who laid waste our land and multiplied our slain." While they were in high spirits, they shouted, "Bring out Samson to entertain us." So they called Samson out of the prison, and he performed for them.

When they stood him among the pillars, Samson said to the servant who held his hand, "Put me where I can feel the pillars that support the temple, so that I may lean against them." Now the temple was crowded with men and women; all the rulers of the Philistines were there, and on the roof were about three thousand men and women watching Samson perform. Then Samson prayed to the Lord, "Sovereign Lord, remember me. Please, God, strengthen me just once more, and let me with one blow get revenge on the Philistines for my two eyes." Then Samson reached toward the two central pillars on which the temple stood. Bracing himself against them, his right hand on the one and his left hand on the other, Samson said, "Let me die with the Philistines!" Then he pushed with all his might, and down came the temple on the rulers and all the people in it. Thus he killed much more when he died than while he lived. - Judges 16:23-30 (NIV)

The Lord is not slow in keeping his promise, as some understand slowness. Instead, he is patient with you, not wanting anyone to perish, but everyone to come to repentance. -   2 Peter 3:9 (NIV)

Day 5

Three Progressive Benefits Of Waiting On The Lord

For the past four days you have been reading (Isaiah 40:31 NIV), and today I want to zone in on some truths in this powerful verse. There are many stages in the waiting process, and we started off talking about an expectant mother that once she gets the news of her baby being on the way, she prepares. As time goes by, her body changes, and every few weeks she must go to the doctor for her checkups to ensure that the seed deposited in her is growing healthy and strong, she gets glimpses of her baby on sonogram pictures, and she gets to hear the heartbeat. These signs of life give the mother hope, joy, and strength to keep going. As the baby grows, she also grows, and things are not as easy or comfortable as it was when she started off, sleeping becomes hard, frequent trips to the bathroom day and night, lower back pain, swollen legs and ankles and heartburn, and exhaustion from carrying the extra weight. But in all her discomfort, she loves that baby; she looks forward to the baby being born even though it is causing her discomfort in the present. The waiting time for a pregnant woman may seem long, but waiting until the due date is a great blessing because that full-term baby will be born developed and healthy most times. So too with a seed that contains the promise and the harvest, sometimes, the promise seems to cause us the most pain, and it may seem to take a long time, and we want to give up but giving up will only cause the harvest to be premature or aborted altogether.

I want to share with you three stages in the waiting process hoping you will change your perspective while you wait for your harvest.

1. A Renewed Mind (Inner Strength)

"But those who wait for the Lord [who expect, look for, and hope in Him] shall change and renew their strength and power]" - (Isaiah 14:31a NIV)

When we learn how to wait on the promises of the Lord and as we meditate on him and his character our thoughts will change from the negatives to the goodness and faithfulness of the promise keeper (Jesus). We will be changed from the inside out –

"Do not be conformed to this world (this age), [fashioned after and adapted to its external, superficial customs], but be transformed (changed) by the [entire] renewal of your mind [by its new ideals and its new attitude], so that you may prove [for yourselves] what is the good and acceptable and perfect will of God, even the thing which is good and acceptable and perfect [in His sight for you]." - Romans 12:2 (AMPC).

2. You will operate in the Supernatural (Moving up Strength)

"they shall lift their wings and mount up [close to God] as eagles [mount up to the sun]"- (Isaiah 14:31b AMPC)

As you become confident in God to keep his Word, He will endow you with supernatural strength to overcome all obstacles that will arise –

"Even as it is written, For Thy sake we are put to death all the day long; we are regarded and counted as sheep for the slaughter.

Yet amid all these things we are more than conquerors and gain a surpassing victory through Him Who loved us." - Romans 8:36-37 (AMPC)

3. You can throw of heavyweights in the Natural (Moving on Strength)

"they shall run and not be weary, they shall walk and not faint or become tired." - (Isaiah 40:31c NIV)

God will infuse you with physical strength when you wait, expect, and look with joy to him to fulfill what He has promised you –

"I have strength for all things in Christ Who empowers me [I am ready for anything and equal to anything through him Who infuses inner strength into me; I am self-sufficient in Christ's sufficiency]." -

Philippians 4:13 (AMPC)

Today I pray that as your wait on the Lord you will be renewed like the eagle!

"Patience is like good motor oil. It doesn't remove all the contaminants. It just puts them into suspension, so they don't get into your works and seize them up. Patient people have, so to speak, a large crankcase. They can put a lot of irritants into suspension." - Cornelius Plantinga

DAILY SCRIPTURES FOR MEDITATION

But those who hope in the Lord will renew their strength. They will soar on wings like eagles; they will run and not grow weary, they will walk and not be faint. - Isaiah 40:31 (NIV)

Consider it a sheer gift, friends when tests and challenges come at you from all sides. You know that under pressure, your faith-life is forced into the open and shows its true colors. So don't try to get out of anything prematurely. Let it do its work, so you become mature and well-developed, not deficient in any way. - James 1:2 - 4 (MSG)

The Lord is not slow in keeping his promise, as some understand slowness. Instead, he is patient with you, not wanting anyone to perish, but everyone to come to repentance. - 2 Peter 3:9 (NIV)

Reflections

Plan 20

WORDS! THEY BECOME YOU

===

You will discover the supernatural power that's unleashed in learning to say what God has told you to say and you will find that by changing your words, you will change your life...but it is YOUR choice, how will YOU choose?

Day 1

What are Words?

In the beginning [before all time] was the Word (Christ), and the Word was with God, and the Word was God Himself (John 1:1 AMP).

From the above Scripture, the Greek word for "word" is logos, and it means "a word, speech, divine utterance, analogy and is preeminently used of Christ, expressing the thoughts of the Father through the Spirit." I know you might be wondering why all this "Greek," but lies the principle of life and creativity. Logos denotes "the expression of thought," and by the expression of God's thoughts, we see the world as we know it. God created everything good, and he did it all by the "*Logos*"—Christ.

What did Jesus say about Words?

Let us look at the words of Jesus...He said, "It is the Spirit who gives life; the flesh profits nothing. The words that I speak to you are spirit, and they are life" (John 6:63 NKJV). From this Scripture, we can clearly establish there are "life" words, and there are "death" words, and Jesus emphatically establishes that his words are "spirit" and "life." But whether the words are "life" words or "death" words, both are "Spirit" words.

We don't see words when we speak them, but yet they can create or destroy as we don't see angels or demons unless they manifest through a tangible body—it's the same way words work. They exist in the spirit form, until manifestation—be it life or death.

In the same way, "death" words empower the enemy, so "life" words empower the angels of God and once we voice our thoughts we give them permission to manifest!

Prayer of Creative Words: *Father, I understand that Jesus is the Logos and by Him, everything was created. Therefore, I will not speak idle words but I will speak creative words.*

DAILY SCRIPTURES FOR MEDITATION

By faith we understand that the universe was formed at God's

command, so that what is seen was not made out of what was visible.
- Hebrews 11:3 (NIV)

The Spirit gives life; the flesh counts for nothing. The words I have
spoken to you—they are full of the Spirit[a] and life. - John 6:63 (NIV)

Day 2

Speaking Is A Choice...Where Does Real Power Lie?

As we look around the world, it seems as if our minds are trained to believe that power lies in the hands of governments and nations, or the rich and famous, or maybe the educated, or even with a particular race of people.

Clearly, we have missed it somewhere, by believing that power lies in possessions, status, and abundance...when truly, from Scriptures, we can see that real power lies in words and ultimate power is resident in God's words. Let us examine a little further on what the Scriptures say, Death and life are in the power of the tongue, and they who indulge in it shall eat the fruit of it [for death or life] (Proverbs 18:21 AMP).

It is very clear from this Scripture; we have a choice in the matter of our words. King Solomon was trying to tell us that the words we speak are shaping the course of our lives, and they will determine if we have a wonderful long life, or if it will be a life of slow poisoning. In the natural life, we must first hear words and those words get into us, and then those words form a belief system by which we live. Now, out of the very words we've heard, or the belief system we adapt to, we then speak out words to create our lives. I am convinced that the type of life we enjoy hinge on the concept of words, and though many words have gone out in the past over your life, I want you to know it is not too late to make a change in the way you speak.

Prayer of Creative Words: *Father, today I understand where the real power lies, and it is not in how much I own, my status or my position in society, but the real power lies in the tongue. With this understanding, I decree and declare a change in my speaking pattern.*

DAILY SCRIPTURES FOR MEDITATION

Death and life are in the power of the tongue, and they who indulge in it shall eat the fruit of it [for death or life] - (Proverbs 18:21 AMP).

For, Whoever would love life and see good days must keep their tongue from eviland their lips from deceitful speech. 1 Peter 3:10 (NIV)

Day 3

The Tongue Is Small But Most Powerful

Most of us don't realize how powerful that part of our body is. The Apostle James calls the tongue a "little" member, yet he associates it with such epic destruction.

The tongue is used to speak words, and once they are sent out, it will produce something- be it good or bad. When I look back at my life, I can remember so many scenes where the most hurt I felt and the most hurt I inflicted was through words.

You cannot have thoughts unless you first hear words. The words you hear form pictures or images in your mind and become what you think about. What "you think about you" will be expressed through words, and finally your words will create the outcome.

A perfect person is not someone that has no flaws, but a perfect person, according to the Bible, is one that is mature in speech because they understand that speaking by the Spirit will create God thoughts and the God thoughts will, in turn, result in mature choices.

When we learn to master the art of expressing our thoughts through the Spirit, we would be on the road to perfecting our lives in every area. We would be dominating our bodies, instead of it dominating us, we will no longer be giving into every sensual desire, but we would be learning how to curb, and eventually control that corrupt, sinful nature.

I challenge you today to ask the Holy Spirit to help you to speak and express thoughts by his power.

Prayer of Creative Words: *Father, today I have come to the understanding that my tongue is small and if not managed by the Holy Spirit can cause much destruction. I do not desire to cause harm or destruction to my life, so I am yielding my tongue to you. Please take control of the words I speak.*

DAILY SCRIPTURES FOR MEDITATION

We all stumble in many ways. Anyone who is never at fault in what they say is perfect, able to keep their whole body in check. - James 3:

2 (NIV)

The tongue also is a fire, a world of evil among the parts of the body. It corrupts the whole body, sets the whole course of one's life on fire, and is itself set on fire by hell.

All kinds of animals, birds, reptiles and sea creatures are being tamed and have been tamed by mankind, but no human being can tame the tongue. It is a restless evil, full of deadly poison.

With the tongue we praise our Lord and Father, and with it we curse human beings, who have been made in God's likeness. Out of the same mouth come praise and cursing. My brothers and sisters, this should not be. - James 3:6-10(NIV)

Day 4

Words Can Heal The Past

We all have a past, and in the world, I wish I could say that everyone experiences a past full of wonderful memories with pictures of rainbows and roses. Unfortunately, this is not the majority of people's past. I have found that the majority of the present plagues in life find their roots in the past and so many cannot let go of it. One of the major weapons of the enemy is to use our past negative experiences to hinder the present and the future.

I have learned that in order to change my life, I must first change my mind about my life.

Unless you have something stronger and more powerful to replace the negatives in your life, it will always remain, and nothing is more powerful and potent than God's words.

God's words create a new picture or vision in our minds and the new pictures or visions then translate into words we speak; thereby changing the whole trajectory of life.

Prolonged ignoring of past hurts opens the door to long-term bitterness, anger issues, health problems, un-forgiveness, and even hatred.

When you get free from negative words and opinions, and you replace them with God's words, there will be no stopping you in fulfilling God's purposes and plans for your life.

The ways we heal our past is by confronting it, accepting responsibility for it, and then speak life into our future! God's patterns are accurate, so it would do us a world of good to follow them.

Prayer of Creative Words: *Father, I come to you, today, recognizing my past, and I need your help in healing my past. I have not been able to move forward because I have refused to deal with my past. I have blamed everyone around me for the hurts and pains, but today, Lord, I am confronting my past with your help.*

DAILY SCRIPTURES FOR MEDITATION

Keep this Book of the Law always on your lips; meditate on it day and night, so that you may be careful to do everything written in it. Then you will be prosperous and successful. - Joshua 1:8 (NIV)

And so, somehow, attaining to the resurrection from the dead. Not that I have already obtained all this, or have already arrived at my goal, but I press on to take hold of that for which Christ Jesus took hold of me. Brothers and sisters, I do not consider myself yet to have taken hold of it. But one thing I do: Forgetting what is behind and straining toward what is ahead, I press on toward the goal to win the prize for which God has called me heavenward in Christ Jesus. - Philippians 3:11a-14 (NIV)

Day 5

Expect Miracles When God Asks A Question

God presents a question to the prophet Ezekiel, but God is all knowing, so why would he need to ask a question? God does not ask questions because he doesn't know the answer, but he asks questions to get us to think and reason outside of the box of the natural—entering the realm of the kingdom, where the impossible becomes possible. He asks us questions to stretch our faith.

The prophet, Ezekiel, had a vision from the Lord, and in this vision, he was led out into the valley of dry bones; it was a representation of the state that the people of Israel were in. But God dares to ask Ezekiel "Son of man, can these bones live?" Ezekiel 37:3 (AMP) and the answer from Ezekiel were beautiful, "O Lord God, You know!" It shows the level of confidence he has in God's abilities. I am sure Ezekiel thought to himself, this is impossible, but if God sees fit to ask this question, then there has to be a way it can be done, and he releases his trust and faith in God for the rest of the instructions.

God may not be asking you about an army of men's dry bones, but the bones are a representation of the things you value and cherish in life that has died on you. God caused Ezekiel to walk through the midst of the dry bones because he wanted Ezekiel to have a clear picture of the situation at hand. You see, before we can give a faith answer to God, we must first be aware of what the problem is. One thing I have also come to understand is that no matter what area of dry bones you are dealing with in your life, the principle of solving them all starts the same way- by speaking!

Prayer of Creative Words: *Father, I will not run away anymore from the issues and dry bones in my life, but like Ezekiel, I stand in the valley trusting You in this process. Yes, I am a bit scared, but I know that if You ask me a question, it is because you already know the answer, and I will follow the way you are leading in this valley.*

DAILY SCRIPTURES FOR MEDITATION

The hand of the LORD was on me, and he brought me out by the

Spirit of the LORD and set me in the middle of a valley; it was full of bones. He led me back and forth among them, and I saw a great many bones on the floor of the valley, bones that were very dry. He asked me, "Son of man, can these bones live?"
I said, "Sovereign LORD, you alone know." - Ezekiel 37:1-3(NIV)

Reflections

_____
_____
_____
_____
_____
_____
_____
_____
_____
_____
_____
_____
_____
_____
_____
_____
_____
_____
_____
_____
_____
_____

BIBLIOGRAPHY

Websites

Anderson, Scott. "You Can Determine What You Value by Where You Spend Your Time." The Huffington Post, TheHuffingtonPost.com, 24 Nov. 2015, www.huffingtonpost.com/scott-anderson/you-can-determine-what-yo_b_8636620.html.

"EliYah.com Ministries." EliYah.com Ministries, www.eliyah.com/.

"Follow Boldly." Daily Devotional from Truth For Life, www.truthforlife.org/resources/daily-devotionals/12/28/1922/.Vujicic,Nick "Life Without Limits"

Griffin, R. Morgan. "10 Health Problems Related to Stress That You Can Fix." WebMD, WebMD, www.webmd.com/balance/stress-management/features/10-fixable-

GotQuestions.org. "What Is Phileo Love?" GotQuestions.org, 4 Jan. 2017, www.gotquestions.org/phileo-love.html.

Henry, Matthew. "Matthew Henry Complete Bible Commentary Online." Bible Study   Tools, www.biblestudytools.com/commentaries/matthew-henry-complete/.

""Hindsight+Is+20/20." Urban Dictionary, https://www.urbandictionary.com/define.php?term=Hindsight+is+20%2F2 0

https://www.christianquotes.info/#axzz4xg5b9C8j

http://www.dictionary.com/

https://www.goodreads.com/

http://www.thomasedison.com/quotes.html

"HuffPost - Breaking News, U.S. and World News." The Huffington Post, TheHuffingtonPost.com, www.huffingtonpost.com/2014/09/28/

Ichykoo, /. "Eros to Agape." Eros to Agape, fromerostoagape.wordpress.com/.

Jackson, Wayne and Steve Lloyd. "Some Great Needs: An Interview with Wayne   Jackson. "Christian Courier, www.christiancourier.com/articles/1263-some-great- needs-an-interview-with-wayne-jackson

Jewish Magazine. The Meaning of Love, as Understood from Hebrew Language, www.jewishmag.com/20mag/hebrew/hebrew.htm.

"Kutless Lyrics." Kutless Lyrics - What Faith Can Do, www.alivelyrics.com/k/kutless/whatfaithcando.html.

Love of Righteousness (Forerunner Commentary), www.bibletools.org/index.cfm/fuseaction/Topical.show/RTD/cgg/ID/7590/Love-Righteousness.htm.

Marshals, Ron. "How Many Ads Do You See in One Day? Get Your Advertising   Campaigns Heard." Red Crow Marketing, 3 Aug. 2017, www.redcrowmarketing.com/2015/09/10/many-ads-see-one-day/

Slick, Matt. "Christian Apologetics & Research Ministry." What Is Prayer?, Matt Slick, July 2017, carm.org/what-prayer

UCSB Science Line, scienceline.ucsb.edu/getkey.php?key=169.

Winner, Jay. "About The Author." Stress Remedy, stressremedy.com/author/.
http://www.yourdictionary.com/identity

Books

Anderson, Neil T., and David Park. Righteous Pursuit. Harvest House Publishers, 2000.

Bengtson, Michelle. Hope Prevails: Insights from a Doctor's Personal Journey through   Depression. Revell, 2016.

Bevere, John. Good or God?: Why Good without God Isn't Enough. Messenger I   International, Inc., 2015.

Keller, Timothy. The Reason for God: Belief in an Age of Skepticism. Penguin, 2016.

Leaf, Caroline. Who Switched off My Brain?: Controlling Toxic Thoughts and Emotions.   Switch On Your Brain, 2009.

Singh, Lisa. Words: They Become You. Inspirations by Lisa, LLC, 2015

Singh, Lisa. Created on Purpose for Purpose Manifesting Your God Purpose. Inspirations by Lisa, LLC, 2015

Stanley, Charles F. "Your Potential Is the Sum of All the Possibilities God Has for Your   Life." How to Reach Your Full Potential for God: Never Settle for Less than His Best, Thomas Nelson, 2009.

Vine, W. E., and W. E. Vine. Vine's Concise Dictionary of Bible Words. Nashville: T. Nelson, 1999. ebook

ABOUT THE AUTHOR

Lisa Singh is the pastor of
Heavenly Grace Ministries in New York and the
bestselling author of Created on Purpose for
Purpose and Words, They Become You.
She is the host of Living the POP Life— People
of Prayer believing in the Power of Prayer...
aired weekdays on www.globespanradio.com
Lisa lives in Queens, NY with her husband and
two children.

www. hgmny.org

Made in the USA
Lexington, KY
17 September 2018